Hard

The story of the watermill and its local community at the heart of Harwood Township in the ancient Parish of Bolton-le-Moors

Former Kiln Annexe of Hardy Mill and Heaton's Cottage c1960

J FREDERICK HORRIDGE

JUNE 2001

No 22 Hardy Cornmill
J F Horridge
Published by Turton Local History Society
June 2001
ISBN 978-1-904974-22-2
Reprinted 2021

TURTON LOCAL HISTORY SOCIETY

This publication is the twenty second issued by the Society, with the aim of promoting an interest in history in general, and Turton in particular, by discussion, research and record.

The main area of interest of the Society covers the old Urban District of Turton which includes the ancient Townships of Bradshaw, Harwood, Longworth, Entwistle, Edgworth, Quarlton and Turton.

The book is reproduced here in electronic format. Only the introductory pages and the inner covers have been significantly changed to bring the layout and information regarding the Society up to date since 2001. Otherwise the text and illustrations remain the same.

Meetings of Turton Local History Society are now (2021) held at 7.30 pm on the fourth Wednesday of each month except for December. Talks and slide shows are held in the Longsight Community Centre, Harwood, Bolton. A series of guided summer evening walks are held in the months of May, June and July. Non members are welcome.

CONTENTS Page

APPENDICES

REFERENCES

ILLUSTRATIONS

Figure 1 Early form of Quern-stone. Probably Iron Age Romano British. Found in the garden of a house in Bradshaw Road, Harwood in 1963.

Chapter I INTRODUCTION

Some 10,000 years ago when man ceased his nomadic wanderings and started to cultivate cereal plants for food, he found it necessary to devise some means of reducing the corn of the cereals into meal or flour.

His first effort was a hollowed rock in which the seeds were pounded with a hammer stone. This later developed into the saddle-stones which consisted of a saucer-shaped bedstone on which the grain was ground with a smaller cylindrical rubbing stone. The next stage was the development of the hand mill or quern which was normally operated by two women and common in biblical times: *'two women shall be grinding at the mill'*. (NT St Matthew)

Each development enabled more ground corn to be produced in less time and with less effort. The quern (Figure 1) was an important advancement in that it ground (or milled) the seeds by rotation of the upper of two round horizontal stones with a handle at the perimeter. This upper stone had a central hole for feeding in the grain, and the bedstone was convexed to shed the ground meal or flour. The quern later progressed into the animal powered mill or gin (thus engine) turned by an ass or ox (or slave!); then the watermill, and later still the windmill.

This book tells the story of one such water driven cornmill which gave its name to the present Hardy Mill Road in Harwood, a Township in the Ancient Parish of Bolton le Moors in the County Palatine of Lancashire. The mill was located on the north side of the road where the bungalow No 83 now stands, and was a working concern from about 1580 to 1830. It is shown on Yates's map of Lancashire of 1786 with the symbol of a toothed wheel (Figure 2).

There were many other watermills in the surrounding districts. Ainsworth, Bradshaw, Turton and Smithills all had their own cornmills which are also indicated on Yates's Map, and there is a record of a mill in Breightmet as far back as 1257 (R1). Harwood also had a water driven fulling mill (or walk mill) for cleansing and felting cloth, and there were similar mills in Bradshaw and Darcy Lever. Local names survive which suggest the siting of other former watermills such as Millwell Lane and Water Millock.

A social change was brought about by the development of the cornmill which provided a service to the community rather than to a single household. It became the hub of activity in the township and a meeting point for those who grew the corn and those who baked the daily bread.

In the following chapters we will first of all examine the development of the Township of Harwood in which Hardy Cornmill played such a vital and necessary role for some two and a half centuries.

Figure 2 Harwood from Yates's Map of 1786

The first modern map of the County Palatine of Lancaster showing mail & cross roads, rivers & canals, mills, coalpits & othe industrial features. Surveyed by William Yates and engraved by Thomas Billinge. The Harwood boundary and hatching of the common areas have been added. Hardy Mill is indicated as a toothed wheel in the centre of Harwood.

Chapter II THE DEVELOPMENT OF HARWOOD TOWNSHIP

A thousand years ago the hilly, inaccessible territory between the rivers Ribble and Mersey in northwest England was largely forest, scrub and mossland. The area was one of the most thinly populated in the kingdom with probably only a thousand or so inhabitants, mainly of Anglo-Saxon or Norse origin. There were no monastic houses in the region, but the people were mostly of the Christian faith and at least ten churches were situated in the scattered townships; it is claimed that Saxon churches were initially sited at the locations of both the Bolton and Deane Parish Churches.

The whole of England south of the Mersey and Humber had by this time been structured with a Shire and Hundredal system almost as today, but with the borders of the ancient kingdoms still preserved. Occupying roughly the western half of England above the Rivers Thames and Avon was the Kingdom of Mercia. The River Mersey was formerly the northern boundary (Maerc- boundary. Ea- river) but after the Battle of Brunanburgh in 937, the kingdom was extended up to the River Ribble. One result of this was the placing of the Mersey/Ribble region under the Mercian Diocese of Lichfield where it remained for the next six centuries. Cheshire was the most northerly county in Mercia and also the last to be established c980.

Soon after the Norman Conquest, William I simplified the existing Anglo-Saxon feudal structure and established the principle that all land in the kingdom was held of the Crown. He granted about half of the land directly to some 180 Great Barons (tenants-in-chief), and the remainder was held by the religious houses or retained as Royal demesne. To fulfil their lease obligations of military or other services, these direct tenants enfeoffed parcels of their estates to sub-tenants, who in turn sub-enfeoffed smaller areas to the knights and thegns.

Roger de Poitou, William's second cousin, was granted the land between the Ribble and Mersey in 1071 after quelling revolts in the north, and he later acquired Amounderness with other land *'beyond the sands'*, thus holding the whole area of the future Lancashire for the latter part of the 11th century.

In the Domesday Survey of 1086, the land *'inter Ripam et Mersham'* was still included with Cheshire, and returned under six administrative Hundreds. The region was only briefly recorded, but particulars of the holdings of the Crown and various thegns were given, and also some numbers of the villeins, bordars, oxmen and serfs. These were the bondsmen tied lifelong to the manors to work the land and carry out everyday duties, and at the time represented over half of the population.

After a rebellion in 1102, Roger de Poitou forfeited all his English estates to Henry I and the region between the Ribble and Mersey became held directly of

Figure 3 Land between Ribble and Mersey c1100, showing location of Harwood Township in Salford Hundred.

the crown by five great tenants-in-chief. The largest of these tenures was the Manor of Manchester which had been inherited by Albert Grelley about 1093. Along with other estates, he held some 90,000 acres in Salford Hundred by the service of 5½ knights. The estate extended roughly from Anglezarke to Ashton-under-Lyne and Harwood (including Bradshaw) was positioned on the north-eastern flank. (Figure 3).

By the time of the Great Inquest in 1212 (R2), Lancashire (or Lancaster) had become established and was returned as a separate county. The districts of Turton, Harewood, Eggewrthe and Hennetwisel were included in this inquiry under the Hundred of Salfordshire. Harewood was recorded as being held jointly at one sixth of a knight's service (R3) by Roger de Samlesbury and Alexander de Harwood. Later in the 1200s, however, the townships of Harwood and Bradshaw became divided with the local family of Bradshaws establishing themselves as Lords of the Manor in the northern half of the region. Harwood, on the other hand, never had the distinction of a resident Lordship.

During the next three centuries the de Harwood portion of Harwood was passed between several families including the Hollands, the Stanleys and the Traffords, whilst the de Samlesbury portion descended through the D'Ewias's, the Southworths, the Gerards and the Ainsworths. By the mid 1500s it would appear that a little over half the area of the township was held by the Traffords, a further quarter was held by the Ainsworths and Stanleys, and the remaining quarter was common land.

The Trafford family from Stretford date back to the 900s and held lands in Harwood from about 1300. Edmund Trafford later acquired by marriage the Manor of Barton-upon-Irwell, (Trafford Park). By a Final Concord (R4) of August, 1589 (A1) Edmund and his father transferred to Nicholas Mosley, citizen and clothmaker of London, *'32 messuages, 32 tofts, 32 gardens, one water mill, 300 acres of land, 100 acres of meadow, 300 acres of pasture, 1000 acres of moor, 1000 acres of heath and heather and 1000 acres of mossland, etc, in Edgworth, Harwood and Barton'* for a consideration of £300. (probably all very approximate areas)

The Mosleys, from Moseley near Wolverhampton, had their Manchester seat at Hough End Hall in Wythington. After amassing great wealth as woollen merchants, Nicholas Mosley purchased the Manor of Manchester in 1592 for £30,000. Three years later he was knighted after serving as Lord Mayor of London. By an Indenture of May 1612, (R5) Sir Nicholas and his son, Edward, the Attorney General of the Duchy of Lancaster, conveyed *'in consideration of eleven hundred pounds ... all that the manor or Lordship of Harwood with all and singular .., messuages, mylles, tofts, crofts, cottages, lands,'* etc to a partnership of five yeomen of Harwood in the Parish of Bolton-le-Moors.

After the Black Death in 1349, when the population was reduced by over one third, the tied villeins and serfs gradually procured freedom status and by 1600 there were no bondsmen left. During this period feudalism declined and when contracts between lord and tenant became customary, the yeomen farmers, who had by that time gained an important position in local society, started to buy the freeholds of the properties in their occupation.

It was obviously the object of the trust partnership of five yeomen of Harwood, namely Matthew Harrison, Henry Haworth, Raufe Higson, Lawrence Horrocks and Edward Greenhalgh (R6), to convey the various properties and lands to the occupants, including themselves. The tenants of the manor were to pay *'a rateable and proportional part of the purchase money if so minded'* for acquisition of *'certain messuages and lands in the hands of occupiers belonging to the manor of Harwood'*. In some cases, when the tenant was without the means, the holding would be purchased as an investment and leased back to the occupant. The conveyances were evidently complete by about 1620.

The Bolton Parish Church Registers of 1573-1660 include many entries for the five yeomen trustees and their families, and for the other principal families who resided in Harwood at that time; Aspinall, Bridge, Brooke, Bromiley, Crompton, Davenport, Entwistle, Fogg, Grundy, Hardy, Haslam, Holmes, Holt, Horridge, Hough, Isherwood, Knowles, Lomax, Mitchell, Nabbs, Roscoe, Sanderson, Singleton, Tonge and Wolfenden. These are the modern spellings for the names which varied considerably in the early registers. Many of the names are included in the various Tax and Protestation Returns for Harwood (R7) and it is to some of these occupants that the tenanted properties must have been conveyed.

From the study of early maps and deeds it has been possible to formulate an impression of Harwood as it was in the early 1600s. Figure 4 shows the natural watercourse boundaries of the Blackshaw, Roading, Riding Gate and Bradshaw Brooks with the assumed folds, farmsteads and road pattern at the time. The presumed areas held by the Ainsworths and Stanleys are shown in the eastern half and south-west corner of the district. The *'highways'* are generally located in the common areas and the present roadways of Longsight Lane, Longsight and Tottington Road had still to be developed.

Five Indentures from the early 1600s have been located but unfortunately the properties were not identified at the time. However, it is almost certain that, as a proportion of the £1100 purchase price for Harwood manor, Henry Haworth paid £160 for Knotts in 1613. Henry Ashurst (as assignee for John Entwistle) paid £113 for Heights in 1613, Edward Greenhalgh paid £74 for Greenhalgh Fold in 1617 and Giles Aynesworth and John Brooke paid £38 and £32 for the two Brookfold Farms in 1615 (R8).

Some of the 200 or so inhabitants of the township would have lived and worked in the various folds and farmsteads but there were groups of cottages around the edge of the commons at Bottom o'th' Moor, Side o'th' Moor, Riding Gate, etc, to accommodate the seventy households estimated from the Hearth Tax returns. The only *'industrial'* premises was the water powered Hardy Cornmill which should have been capable of catering for this number of households with some farmers possibly taking their grain to neighbouring cornmills to be ground. A manorial fulling mill was later recorded in 1630 at *'Labbys'* on the Harwood side of Bradshaw Brook (R9).

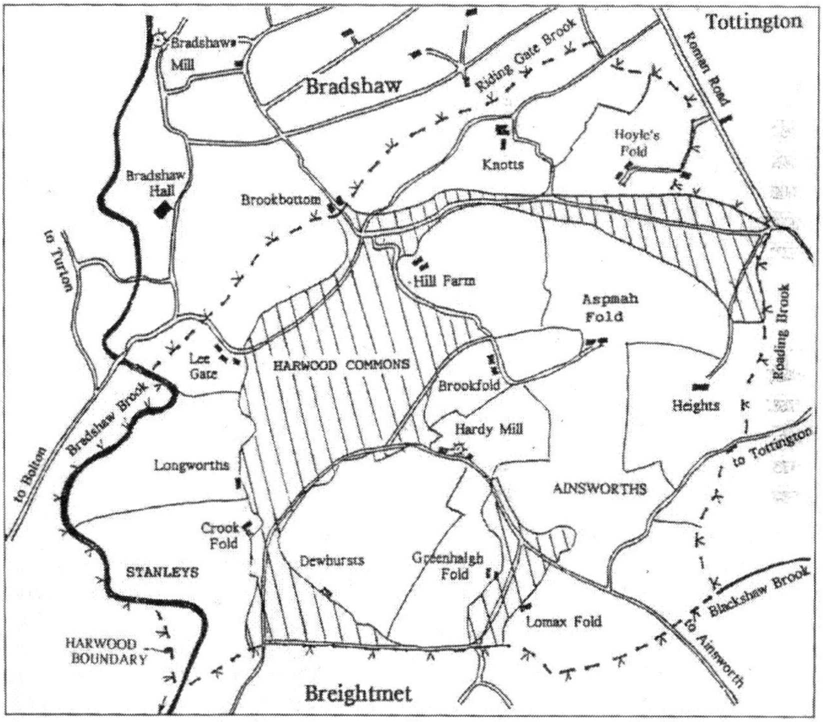

Figure 4 Presumed Plan of Harwood c1612

It is interesting to reflect on the times when the manor of Harwood was undergoing the above restructuring. This was a very cruel and unsettled period between the end of the Elizabethan Age and the outbreak of the Civil War with such notable events as the Gunpowder Plot in 1605, the emigration of the Pilgrim Fathers to New England in 1620, and more locally, the public hanging of nine Lancashire Witches at Gallows Hill, Lancaster in 1612. In the Manchester Constables Accounts for Michaelmas, 1616 is recorded: *'13th Marche. Item paide for Whippinge Elizabeth Romesden of Harwoodd for Filchinge. 4d'.*

Figure 5 Dounby Mill, North Mainland, Orkney.

Chapter III WATER MILLS IN BRITAIN

Whilst credit must go to the Greeks for the evolution of the first water driven wheel in the latter days of their Era, it is to the Romans that we are beholden for the introduction of the watermill into Britain.

In the Roman Empire, the previously mentioned hand mills or querns were in general use by households, but to provide the considerable amounts of meal required to feed the armies, larger mills were needed. Slave labour and animal power being plentiful, these were mainly used as a means of turning the heavier millstones. When Christianity became the official religion of the Romans early in the fourth century, slavery petered out and the military engineers turned their attention to the construction and improvement of water powered mills. Rome itself was said to be converted to water milling by about 400 AD.

Cornmilling in the Province of Britain followed a somewhat similar pattern and several remains of watermills dating back to the latter part of the occupation have been unearthed mainly along Hadrian's Wall. The Romans understood and used the principles of gearing to turn horizontal millstones with their vertical water wheels. After their exodus from Britain, a general stagnation in craftsmanship and commerce set in, and this lasted until the arrival of the Angles and Saxons, who in the last quarter of the first millennium resumed the construction of watermills on a large scale.

Up in the Northern Islands of Scotland, where Roman influence was never experienced, the Norse mills were normal. These had horizontal water wheels with a direct vertical drive to the millstones, and were generally small mills positioned directly over a stream. The best surviving example of a Norse mill is the beautifully preserved Dounby Mill on Orkney (Figure 5).

The Domesday survey of 1086 registered 6086 unclassified mills in the 36 counties covered, but recorded no information on mills between the Ribble and Mersey. William Yates's map of 1786 indicates over 300 watermills of various types in Lancashire, mostly located in the east towards the Pennine range where the streams fall faster.

Although watermills are mostly associated with grinding the corn or grain of cereal plants such as wheat, barley, oats and rye, they were also used to grind other materials such as snuff, mustard, gunpowder and flints. In fact, water power was the initial source of energy that motivated the Industrial Revolution, and over the years, watermills have had numerous commercial uses such as sawing timber, forging iron, grinding minerals, spinning, weaving and fulling textiles, printing, making paper, etc. It is estimated that there have been well over 10,000 of these water driven mills in Britain at one time or another.

Chapter IV MANORIAL MILLS

Under the feudal structure, the manorial system developed in England and the first manors as recorded in the Domesday survey were the residences or farmhouses of middle class members of society. Later the manors became feudal administrative units on large estates which could contain several villages or townships, and not necessarily the lord's residence. By the early 1600s the manor was legally defined as a landed property with the lord exercising rights of jurisdiction and holding private courts.

The most important cornmills at this time were those owned by the manor or monastery to which they were a valuable source of income. The lords usually maintained soke rights, which meant that everyone growing cereals in the manor had to take their corn to the manorial mill to be ground. These rights were never established by statute law (and thus never abolished) but were invariably upheld by the courts, and lawsuits persisted into the 1800s. A local example was Brookfold Farm in Harwood which was leased by William Hulme to the occupant, William Brooke, in 1664 with the proviso: *'as other tenants ... all the grain grown there were to be brought to Oakenbottom Mill to be ground or 10s rent to be paid to Charles, Earl of Derby'* (R 10).

Some of the milling rights granted actually prohibited the tenants from possessing hand mills and allowed for their confiscation by the landowners. One such situation led to a rebellion in 1329 by the local people against Vale Royal Abbey in Cheshire who possessed the milling rights for the nearby Darnhall Cornmill (Figure 6).

Figure 6 Darnhall Cornmill, SW of Winsford, Cheshire. Working until c1980.

The toll for milling was usually regulated by the manor and taken as a fractional part of the ground corn such as a sixteenth or twentieth. This was called the multure and a multure bowl was normally used to extract the toll for storage in the millers bin or ark. As only the miller and his assistants knew how much meal was produced from a given amount of corn, it was an easy matter for them to keep more than was their due. The system created many disputes, often giving the miller's trade a bad name, and the toll was commuted to monetary charges by an Act of 1796.

In the days of feudal Britain, the millers were generally bound to the lord of the manor, but by medieval times, they had started to rent the mills and conduct their own businesses. The leases varied and whilst some required the tenant to maintain the buildings and provide millstones, fuel, etc, others such as at Bradshaw, included maintenance and free coal for the kiln.

The millers later became traders, buying grain from the harvester or market and selling the processed meal, flour and animal feed back to the bakers and stock farmers. Eventually, like the yeomen, they began to buy the leaseholds of the mills, which from then on were often handed down from father to son through several generations. This was the case with Hardy Mill as will be seen when we examine the succession of millers in later chapters.

Figure 7 Hardy Cornmill c1800 (Drawn by Edward Hardy)

Chapter V THE CORNMILL

In the North-west of England, mill buildings were mainly ramshackle affairs and not quite like the picturesque scenes depicted by Constable, They were of a functional layout with two or three storeys and generally constructed in traditional materials following the style of the local farmhouses.

An architect's impression of Hardy Cornmill cl800 contrived from early photographs and maps is shown in Figure 7. The construction of the mill building was customary with walls of random stonework and suspended floors with timber beams, joists and boarding. The roof was clad in stone slates on to timber battens, rafters and purlins.

A drying kiln was usually necessary in the damp climate of Lancashire, and at Hardy Mill, a kiln with sack hoist was added to the front of the mill in the early 1700s (Figure 9). This annexe had solid external walls constructed in hand made bricks on a much thicker random stone plinth wall, and a roof with large timber cross purlins carrying rafters fastened with oak pegs. The kiln would normally have had a suspended floor formed with perforated ceramic tiles on an iron framework and a system of flues and fire box below.

Figure 8 Former Kiln/Cottage of Hardy Mill before restoration in 1971.

The kiln annexe is the only part of the original mill to survive and was later converted into the cottage No 85 Hardy Mill Road. During recent restoration of the building, (Figure 8) there was evidence of several internal flues and the addition of a 9 inch brick cross wall to divide the rooms and support the upper floor. Corn seeds were found in the masonry joints and cavities, and there was an open hole into the hoist shaft.

The construction of a weir was the customary method of directing water from a stream down the head race (or leat) to the waterwheel without obstructing the main current. If the available flow of water was insufficient for continuous working of the mill, it was usual to collect the water into a man-made pond or dam, as was the case at Hardy Mill.

The brook which supplied Hardy Mill surfaces from a spring or land-drain outfall about 750 yards east of the mill adjacent to Harwood Golf Club, at a head of 500 feet above sea level. It originally ran as an open watercourse falling about 100 feet to the mill dam but today it is culverted under Greenwoods Lane and the rear gardens of 99 to 121 Hardy Mill Road. The water catchment area is about 150 acres and stretches up to Bowstone Hill at 800 feet above sea level. It can be calculated that, with an average rainfall, the flow of the stream would fill the mill dam in a day. The miller could stop or control the flow of water to the mill race by a system of sluice gates and also direct surplus water back into the tail race to rejoin the stream. Below Hardy Mill the stream is known locally as Folly Brook and is joined by Asmus Fold Stream & Such Brook. It continues through the Ruins, Harwood Vale and Castlecroft to outfall into Bradshaw Brook.

Waterwheels in the Northwest were invariably vertical of either the overshot or breastshot type. The overshot wheel had buckets or troughs around the rim and the stream of water was channelled via a launder to discharge on to the wheel just past top-centre. Rotation was generated by the weight of water in the buckets coupled with the force of the current. The breastshot wheel was similar to the overshot but with the water being channelled on to the wheel about axle height causing inverse rotation mainly by the weight of water in the buckets.

In 1752/53, John Smeaton, the eminent civil engineer, carried out a series of experiments to test the effectiveness of water powered wheels (also wind powered) and introduced many improvements to their construction. He concluded that the efficiency ratio of the overshot system was 63% and the breastshot 55%.

The wheels and axles were initially made of timber but during the 16th and 17th centuries, as the size of wheels increased, wrought iron was utilized for the buckets, paddles and various jointing straps. The large diameter timber shafts were replaced by smaller wrought iron axles introduced by Smeaton in 1769.

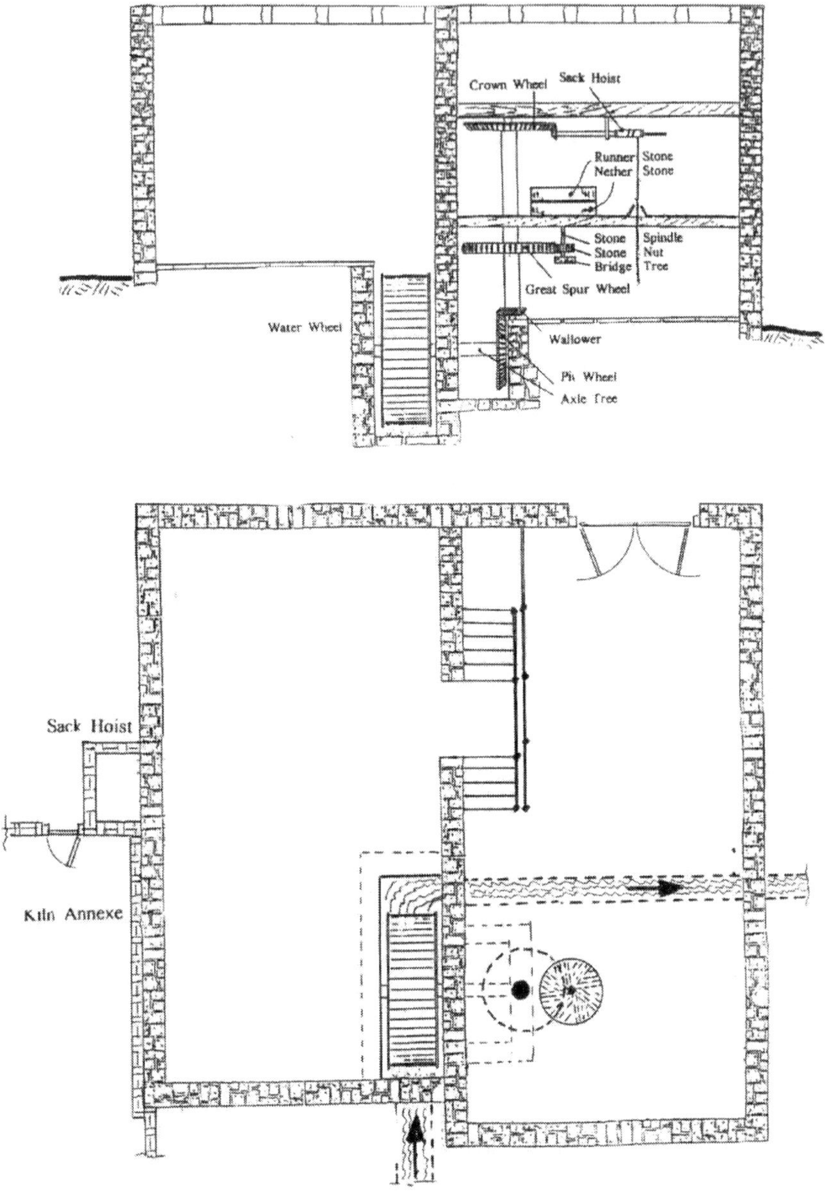

Figure 9 Presumed Plans and Sections of Hardy Cornmill.

Later the wheels were fabricated entirely from wrought or cast iron sections bolted together.

The water drive at Hardy Mill was of the breastshot type with a timber wheel about 8 feet diameter by 2 feet wide and a wrought iron axle of three inches diameter. The remains of the waterwheel and brick housing still exist below ground, having been carefully retained and covered.

There were numerous arrangements of transmission gearing for watermills, but the system most likely operated at Hardy Mill would have been the *'underdrift set'* illustrated in the section of the mill building (Figure 9). The shaft of the water wheel (axle tree) extended into the mill and rotated a large timber or iron bevelled cog wheel (pit wheel). This meshed with a much smaller bevelled pinion (wallower) which had a substantial vertical timber shaft about 18 inch diameter holding a large gear wheel (great spur wheel) beneath the first floor and a similar sized bevelled wheel (crown wheel) at the top.

The great spur wheel propelled a small pinion (stone nut) with a vertical shaft (stone spindle) that passed through to the floor above and turned the upper millstone (runner stone). The stone spindle was held by a toe-bearing and bridge block seated on go a timber beam (bridge tree) which had vertical adjustment at one support for the accurate setting of the small gap between the stones (tentering). The crown wheel drove a small bevelled cog with a horizontal shaft from which the sack hoist was operated.

In the milling operation, the corn, after threshing or winnowing (A2) to *'sort the wheat from the chaff'*, was dried in the kiln and then hoisted up to a hopper from which a chute fed the *'grist to the mill'* through a large hole in the centre of the runner stone. The interfaces of the two stones were dressed with a pattern of radial furrows which trapped and cut the seed as it was forced from the centre to the circumference, The produced meal or flour was collected in a circular casing to the millstones (the tun) from which it was discharged into sacks.

The millstones at Hardy Mill were five feet diameter by one foot thick and several remain in the garden of the bungalow 83 Hardy Mill Road. They were no doubt quarried locally from the millstone grit bedrock, possibly at the quarry at Horrocks Fold, Edgworth, where John Horrocks with his sons, Samuel and John ran a modest business in the late 1700s cutting, dressing and polishing millstones. John junior later became the owner of several cotton mills in the Preston, Chorley and Manchester areas (R11).

Chapter VI THE HARDIES

Little is known of the origins of Hardy Cornmill except for references in two ancient documents. The previously mentioned Final Concord of 1589 between the de Trafford and the Mosley families refers to *'thirty two tofts, one water mill, etc....in Edgworth, Harwood and Barton'*. Also conveyance in 1612 of the manor of Harwood from the Mosleys to the five yeomen refers to *'messuages, mylles and tofts'* In the absence of more positive evidence we can only presume that the watermill referred to was in fact Hardy Mill, and that it was a manorial mill until dispersal of the Harwood tenancies after 1612.

The local cornmills in Bradshaw and Turton and the fulling mills at Bradshaw and Labbys were also manorial mills. An Indenture of 1768 for Old Mans Farm, Greens Arms Road, Turton stipulated that the tenant *'shall bring all the corn, grain and malt...to the water corn mill of the said Edward Chetham to be ground there at the usual toll and multure according to the custom or usage of the Manor or Lordship of Turton'.*

The Hardy family were well established in Harwood during the 1600s with over twenty entries for Hardier, Hardyer, Hardi, Hardie or Hardy in the Bolton Parish Church Registers between 1589 and 1698. With this limited information, a family tree and some of the following observations are somewhat speculative, being largely based on *'circumstantial evidence'.*

Elys Hardier, whose wife died in 1589, was most likely an early miller, leasing the mill and adjacent land from the manor, and Ellis, John and Willyam would be his sons, Willyam, his third son, would be the next miller who purchased the mill and land from the five yeomen of Harwood when aged about 30. He signed the oath in the Protestations of 1641 and paid the tax for two hearths in 1663 and 1664, one hearth probably being for the kiln (R7). His three nephews, Ellis, Will and Ehud are also listed in the 1641 Protestation Returns.

Ellis, the elder of Elys's three sons, was obviously involved in the conveyancing by the five yeomen to the occupiers as he was a witness of the Indenture for John Brooke on January 1st, 1615(16) (Hulme Deed No 109). He was the church warden for Harwood at Bolton Parish Church in 1645 but was not included in the 1664 Hearth Tax Returns.

Thomas (1609-1698), the first son of the above Ellis and nephew of Willyam, probably succeeded his uncle as miller and eventually sold the estate to James Heaton. Thomas had three wives and five children, his last wife being Jane Hopwood who he married in 1670 at the age of 61. He was registered with one hearth in 1664 but not liable for tax.

Thomas's brother, William (1620-1670), was an approved breadbaker and maltster for Harwood in 1653 when the local constables reported to the High Constable: *'Presentments by John Brooke and Henry Ashurst, Cunstables of Harwood as followeth: Wee present William Hardier and James Isherwood Breadbakers for Harwood and the towne hath mett and thinks them fitt to be continewed. And wee present William Hardier also as Maltster to bee continewed by the consent of the towne. And as for Badgers and Droviers wee have none within our division. These presentments are made by us afforesaid the 9th of January, 1653 according to a warrant directed to us for that purpose by the high Cunstables. By us John Brooke, Henry Ashurst, Constables'.*

To summarise, as the name of the mill implies, the Hardy family were without doubt the millers in the early 1600s or before. Possibly Elys, then Willyam and finally Thomas. Probably Willyam purchased the mill and land about 1620 and nephew Thomas sold it some 50 years later but carried on as miller for a time.

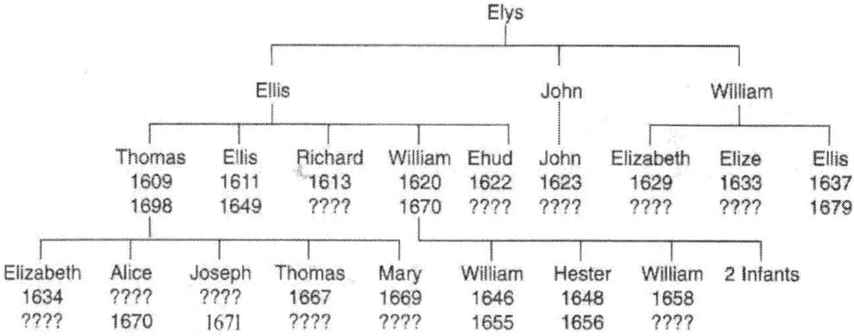

HARDY FAMILY TREE - projected from the following entries for Hardier, Hardyer: Hardi, Hardie and Hardy of Harwood in the earliest Bolton Parish Church Register

BAPTISMS				
Thomas	S of Ellis	25	12	1609
Ellis		19	12	1611
Richard	S of Elize	23	5	1613
William	S of Ellis	7	5	1620
Ehud	S of Elize	21	4	1622
John	S of John	7	4	1623
Elizabeth	D of Willyam	22	2	1629
Elize	S of Willyam	23	3	1633
Elizabeth	D of Thomas	6	7	1634
Ellis	S of Willyam	21	5	1637
William	S of William	28	2	1646
Hester	D of William	30	12	1648
William	S of William	25	1	1658
Thomas	S of Thos & Ann	10	5	1667
Mary	D of Thos & Ann	26	2	1669

BURIALS			
Wife of Elys	5	5	1589
John	29	3	1595
Child of Ellis	25	2	1611
Infant of William	14	7	1634
Infant	14	7	1635
Thomas	2	4	1636
Ellis			1649
Alis wife of Ellis	13	1	1654
Wills of William (pox)	29	9	1655
Hester dau of Will	22	2	1656
William	21	10	1670
Alice dau of Thomas	27	9	1670
Joseph son of Thomas	9	2	1671
Ellis son of Willyam	10	5	1679
Thomas	3	3	1698

Chapter VII THE HEATONS

The Heaton family take their name from the manor of Heton-in-Lonsdale (recorded in Domesday as Hietune) which is situated alongside the River Lune just west of Lancaster. The ancestry of the family can be traced back through nine centuries to a Thegn named Waldef of Ulverston whose first son Augustine acquired the manor of Heton in the last decade of the 1100s (R12 & R13).

From these beginnings the Heaton family spread throughout Lancashire becoming lords of the manor, knights, clergy, lawyers, merchants, yeomen farmers, etc. By the 1300s branches of the family had established themselves in south Lancashire with the acquisitions of the manors of Heton-under-Horwich and Birchley, Billinge along with other lands in Horwich, Rumworth and Lostock which they held for the next two centuries.

About 1490, Richard Heton of Heton and Birchley (c1460-1535) succeeded to the manors and had 4 children with his first wife, Agnes, and 12 with his second wife, Margaret. After his death, this large family unfortunately entered into a succession of disputes and litigation that lasted for 35 years and by 1570, Christopher Anderton, a distant relative and lawyer from Chorley had, by devious means, acquired both the Heton and Birchley estates.

Many members of the Heaton family then found themselves as rent paying tenants rather than owners of their holdings and started to move away to nearby districts. One of the dispersed descendants, William Heaton, died at Adlington in 1619 bequeathing his estate to his son Thomas (1601-1646) who eventually married Ellen Green, an heiress from Abram. The couple settled in Halliwell and had two sons, William and James.

In 1665, the second son of the above union, James (c1640-1721) married Elizabeth Longworth, an heiress of Halliwell, at Deane Parish Church, and they had five children between 1666 and 1679: Thomas, James, Peter, Ellen and Elizabeth. James and his family moved to Harwood in 1676 and two years later he paid six shillings in the Poll Tax recorded as: *'James Heaton with wyfe, two children and maydservant'* (R7). He was obviously financially sound at the time, having inherited, or acquired by marriage, estates in Abram, Adlington and Haslam Hey, Ainsworth, and he bought, probably from the Hardys, the cornmill and adjacent land that eventually was to be known as Heaton's Estate.

It seems most likely that James acquired the mill and land as an investment and also to provide an occupation for his second son, James Jnr (1668-1741) to whom he eventually left all the estate. His first son Thomas graduated at Brazenose College, Oxford, then Christ's College, Cambridge, and eventually became rector of churches in Bedfordshire and Hertfordshire, after having married Anne Maykinsonne at Bolton in 1694.

A detailed survey exists for Heaton's Estate prepared by John Albinson (RI4) in 1824 which gives a plan of the site, names of the fields plus calculations of the areas, and an Abstract of Title. The latter is presented below and gives factual information to enable the story of both Hardy Mill and Heatons Farm to be unfolded from the time of James Heaton's acquisition.

For the next 150 years the mill descended from father to son (or son-in-law) in a direct line through four generations until its closure c1830, and this progression is illustrated in tree form on page 22.

Abstract of the Title of Mr John Kirkman to an Estate called Heatons in Harwood in the County of Lancs. March 31st, 1824

1685 June 25th. From Joshua Lomax of St Albans, Co of Hertford, Esq, to James Heaton of Harwood, Chapman, of all that corn mill, Hardy Mill and closes of land containing 13 Acres which said Lomax had purchased lately from Heaton. Term 1000 yrs. Rent £7.

1686 March. From Jas Heaton to Jas Duckinfield of Penketh Esq and Andrew Crossly of Manchester, Chapman. Heaton owed?... £50 and Crossly £18 and costs in Law.

1693 February 16th. From Wm Heaton of Brindle to said Jas Heaton for £70 and £20 granted said Mill and land to Jas.

1694 May 21st. From Thos Crompton of Bolton, Chapman, to Jas Heaton Jnr recited Heaton on May 16th 1694 assigned premises.

1694 May 16th. Assigned premises to Jno Rothwell of Sharples for £20 and Rothwell by his Will came to said Thos Crompton and Crompton for £ll-10s assigned same to younger Heaton.

1694 October 27th. From Harbart Crossly of Chester, Chapman, John Crossly of Knutsford, Chapman, Executors of Andrew Crossly to James Heaton younger for £22-10s said premises.

1695 November 2nd. Poll from Jas Duckinfield of Bold Esq for £22-10s to said Jas Heaton said premises.

1720 August 2nd. Jas Heaton Elders Will unto Jas Heaton younger. All his lands in Harwood.

1741 February 4th. Jas Heaton of Harwood by his Will gave all his premises to his 7 children share and share alike (except Meadowcroft Heaton Executor ... his son ... one shilling)

1743 August 13th. From Meadowcroft Heaton and 7 other children by agreement stating Will was not properly executed and they agreed for same to be divided as therein mentioned. Meadowcroft Heaton in the penal sum of £1000 and the other portions in same sum.

1744 January 7th. From Meadowcroft Heaton to John Kirkman for £290 did Demise All those Mill Buildings and land and 13 acres of land with two closes called Car and Roy field also 3 acres of land.

1745 May 27th & 28th. From Meadowcroft Heaton of Pilkington, Schoolmaster, to the other seven children for £90 all those 2 acres called Roy field and Car.

1745 May 29th. From Thos Harrison of Birmingham and Martha his wife later Martha Clarke who was Executor of Thos Morrall late Vicar of Bolton (1721-1737) and Thos Shipphard (Bolton Solicitor) his other Executor of 1st part, Meadowcroft and others of 2nd part to Jno Kirkman and others of 3rd part in consideration of £200 for All that mill, several closes of land containing 13 acres also two closes of land called Roy field and Car containing 2 acres.

1745 May 31st. From John Kirkman and sisters to David Heaton in consideration of rent of £7. All two mills, houses, stables and 4 closes of land called Longshut, Ralph Meadow, Lowmost Hardier Car and Clover Hillock about 3 acres of land being 1/3 of all the premises demised by Lomax to Jas Heaton, Grandfather.

1759 March 13th. Will of John Kirkman gave his eldest son Zach premises called Heatons subject to rents etc.

1782 May 21st. From Zach Kirkman to Wm Kennedy of Manchester, merchant, for £250 for 500 years of All those 2 closes of freehold called Roy field and Car and all those other fields called Croft acre, Barn Croft, Meadow, Great Hey and Little Hey containing about 10 Acres after 8 yards (Cheshire Measure R15).

1790 October 19th. From Wm Kennedy and John Kirkman to Ann Crompton of Bolton for £450 assigned over all said premises.

1796 December 12th. From Ann Crompton and John Kirkman to Thos Nuttall of Little Bolton for £450 of all those said premises.

1819 October 21st. From Wm Woods and Jas Lomax, Executors of Thos Nuttall and John Kirkman to Elizabeth Bancroft, widow and Executor of Rev Thomas Bancroft, late Vicar of Bolton (1793-1811) for £1000 for All the aforesaid premises.

Notes:- Agreement 7th January, 1744
Mansion House, Bowkhouse, Barn, Stable, Miln, Kiln and 3 cottages & 13 acres of land: and 2 closes of land called Car and Roy fields about 3 acres

13-0-0
3-0-0

10-0-0

1745 27th & 28th May, Sale of Roy fields and Car - described as being two acres.

The first conveyance in the Abstract of Title is when Joshua Lomax of St Albans sold Hardy Mill and 13 acres of land to James Heaton on the 25th June, 1685. He had *'lately purchased same from Heaton'* and sold it back to him subject to a ground rent of £7 per annum for a term 1000 years. The object of Joshua Lomax in pursuing these transactions will be explained later in Chapter XV.

It is fortunate that there are available from about 1700 the Wills of many of the characters who participate in this history and which give valuable factual information. These include Henry Haworth, Joshua Lomax, James Heaton Snr, James Heaton Jnr, John Lister, Meadowcroft Heaton, David Heaton, Margaret Thweat, James Ormrod, John Walch, David Walch, John Pilling, Charles Hopwood, John Kirkman and Jethro Scowcroft. Other sources of information for the period are the Harwood Enclosure Awards with Map of 1801, the several Land Tax Assessments of the late 1700s to mid 1800s, and various deeds of land and property conveyances.

Some time after purchasing Hardy Mill, James Heaton Snr. encroached on to the Commons immediately to the south-west of his estate to build *'one bay and croft'*. In *'A true survey taken of ye commoning of Harwood'* for the *'Trustholders and Charterers of ye Commons in Harwood in ye parish of Bolton 10th April, 1694'* (R16). James and four others were found guilty of encroachment but it is not known if they were ejected. James apparently ran into financial problems around this time, as the Abstract of Title indicates some mortgaging of the mill and estate involving the Duckinfields, Crosslys, Rothwells, Cromptons and Heatons of Brindle.

James Heaton Jnr was only about seven years old when his father purchased Hardy Cornmill in 1676, and the mill could have been worked for a time by Thomas Hardy until young James was experienced and old enough to take over. Thomas Hardy would have been about 66 years old but he lived on to the great age of 89. Alternatively, some other miller could have been employed such as John Lister of Tonge who married Alice Croichloe of Harwood in 1658 and paid two shillings in the 1678 Poll Tax for Harwood (R7) as *'John Leyster and his wyfe'*. In his Will of April, 1683 he was described as *'a milner'*, but in the *'Inventory of all the goods and chattels both moveable and unmoveable of John Leister late of Harwood and Deceased'*, whilst he owned two looms and several *'meale arkes'*, there are no items included to suggest that he owned a cornmill.

Heaton's residence was built about 1685 on the eastern flank of the estate and acquired by Thomas Crompton, a chapman from Bolton. In 1694 James Heaton Jnr purchased the residence for £22.10s and between then and 1714 he and his wife Margaret had eight children, all baptised at Bolton Parish Church (See lineage of Hardy Mill, page 22).

When James Heaton Snr died in 1721, by his Will he bequeathed *'all those messuages, lands, etc in Adlington which I formerly purchased from my late brother William, deceased, together with all my right, title, etc to that messuage called Height Barn in Haslam Hey, all my estate in Abram, commonly called Heaton House, and all my messuages, etc in Harwood, together with all household goods, etc to my son James Heaton whom I make sole executor'*. The Will was proved at Chester in the same year. He was interred at Bolton Parish Church, as was his wife Elizabeth who died six years later.

This left James Jnr as the sole owner of the mill and several estates. Heaton's residence by this time had been developed into a farmstead with a barn and bowkhouse (R18) and no doubt some of the members of his large family would have been helping to run the cornmill and farm. Eventually his third son, David (1710-1784) took over the role of miller.

James Heaton Jnr died in 1741 and by his Will bequeathed *'unto Chas Jenkinson and Thos Jenkinson of Bury £10 each; to Thomas Booth of Breightmet £20; to Catherine Hope £20. The residue and remainder unto his seven younger children, viz:- to Peter, Rebecka, Elizabeth, Mary, David, Ann and James equally. His eldest son Meadowcroft one shilling, and his wife the interest of all his goods, etc, for life. Margaret his wife and Rebecka his eldest daughter to be Executors'*. The Will was proved at Chester in March, 1741. His Widow Margaret died at Breightmet six years later. Chas Jenkinson, Thomas Jenkinson and Thomas Booth were his grandsons.

DIRECT LINEAGE OF HARDY MILL THROUGH FIVE GENERATIONS

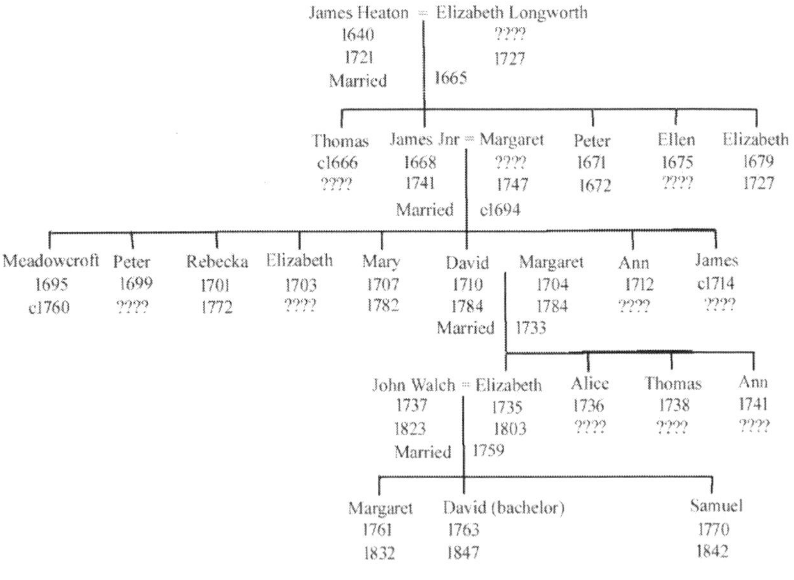

Chapter VIII THE ESTATE DIVIDED

The year 1745 was important to this history in that it was then that Hardy Mill and the Heaton's Farm became divided into two separate holdings. Figure 10 shows the layout of the estate at that time with the names and acreages of the fields. Some conflicting acreages are stipulated in the Abstract of Title but the total area of the original estate was a little over 29 Statute Acres (R15.)

Apart from some encroachment for house building immediately adjacent to Hardy Mill Road, this layout has not altered in the last 250 years and is now the edge of the Green Belt between Bolton and Bury. Figure 12 shows the fields of Great Hey, Croft Acre, Barn Croft, Great Meadow and Little Hey (RI7) as they are today and the field pattern can also be identified in the aerial view of Hardy Mill area (Figure 13).

After the death of James Heaton Jnr in 1741 the estate was left to his eldest son Meadowcroft in trusteeship, which at that time was the normal procedure in family settlements to ensure that the descendants retained their inheritance. In 1743, the widow Margaret must have relinquished her life interest in the estate and a settlement was agreed by the seven children on August 13th of that year with Meadowcroft in trust on a surety of £1000.

Due no doubt to the extended legal and mortgaging transactions involving the executors of Thomas Morrell (late Vicar of Bolton) it took until May, 1745 for Meadowcroft as trustee to dispose of the estate. This was conveyed to Mr John Kirkman and his sisters Hannah and Alice, and included Heaton's residence (Figure 11), the bowkhouse, barn, stable, mill, kiln, three cottages and 29 statute acres of land.

As stated in the previous chapter, William Heaton's third son David had taken up the role of miller and two days after their purchase of the estate the Kirkmans conveyed the mill buildings and adjacent land back to David. They retained Heaton's residence, the bowkhouse, the barn and the upper seven fields of 22 statute acres (named on the plan). The future of Heaton's Farm and the Kirkmans will be continued in Chapter XIV.

David Heaton's portion of the estate consisted of the mill, kiln, mill dam, stables, house and four closes of land containing 7 statute acres. These were the fields adjacent to Hardy Mill named Ralph Meadow, Clover Hillock, Lowmost Hardier Carr and Longshut (unnamed on the plan - locations unknown).

The Abstract of Title for the estate shows that during the transactions, the purchase price to the Kirkmans was reduced from £290 in 1744 to £200 in 1745. It seems that by a prior agreement, David Heaton had no further outlay for his acquired portion of the estate except *'to pay on Whitsunday seven pounds to the*

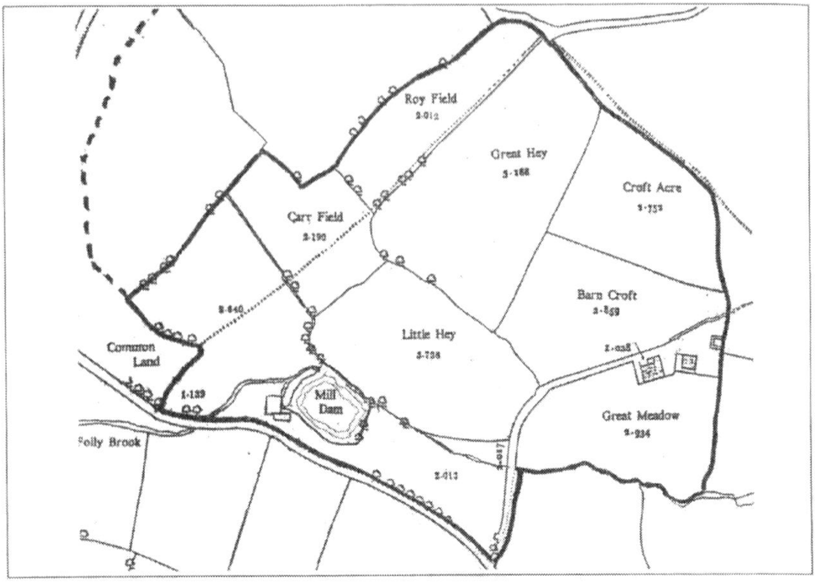

Figure 10 Plan of Hardy Mill and Heatons c1745
Showing Layout, names and Statute Acreages of Fields.

Figure 11 Heaton's Farm c1960.

Figure 12 Field Layout as today. Heaton's Farm is on right.

Figure 13 Aerial Photograph of Hardy Mill Area c1960 looking North.

trustees of Bolton Church yearly and every year with all other taxes, lays or other expenses to which the ground is or maybe subject to'.

The eldest son, Meadowcroft (1695-1760?) was described in the Abstract of Title as a Schoolmaster of Pilkington and he was twice married; first to Elizabeth Fletcher of Ringley in 1722 and later to Ann Isherwood at Bolton in 1755. There were four children from the marriages, John, Charles, Thomas and Margaret. He obviously acquired some land and property by marriage and in his Will of June 1760 (A3), he left to his children the estates of Nabfold, Isherwoods, Harwood Meadows and Old Pit, plus three houses.

David Heaton (1710-1784) had married Margaret (surname omitted in registers) at Bolton Parish Church in 1733 and they had four children in the following eight years, Elizabeth, Thomas, Alice and Ann.

David built another house adjoining the kiln fronting on to what is now Hardy Mill Road which later came to be known as Heaton's Cottage (Figure 14). The datestone reads *'Heaton: David and Margaret: 1757'*. The two cottages 89 and 91 Hardy Mill Road (Figure 15) were built about the same time and Rose Cottage (Figure 16) was built some twenty- five years later.

The mill, as well as grinding the corn for the local farmers, would now be trading in meal, flour and other cereals from local suppliers. The population of Harwood had increased about five times from the estimated 200 inhabitants in 1600, and the output of one cornmill would not be sufficient for this number of people.

Thomas, only son of David and Margaret, would appear to have died at an early age, but the three daughters married and raised 13 grand-children over the next 20 years or so. The youngest Ann, married Dennis Kirkman from the Parish of Middleton in March, 1761 at the age of 20 and they had five children, John, William, James, Thomas and Ann. Alice married James Ormrod in October, 1755 when she was 19 and also had five children, Alice, Mary, George, Ann and Peggy. James was the grandson of Oliver Ormrod of Birches Farm, Bradshaw and a 'second' cousin to Peter (Ready Money) Ormrod who in 1871 donated £4000 to the cost of rebuilding Bolton Parish Church. The eldest daughter, Elizabeth (Betty) married John Walch from Cockey Moor in December, 1760 when they were both 25 years of age and had three children, Margaret, David and Samuel; more of the Walch family in the next chapter.

David Heaton died in September 1784 at the age of 75 and his Will of the previous month (Probate April 1790) gives such detailed information of the Hardy Mill estate and the distribution of the various properties and land to his daughters that it is presented in full:-

Figure 14 Heatons Cottage and Datestone c1965.

Figure 15 Front and Rear Views of Cottages 89 & 91 Hardy Mill Road c1910.

'I give and bequeath to my daughter Elizabeth Walch, the wife of John Walch, to their heirs, executors or assigns, the house adjoining to the Mill, the Mill, the Kiln, the coal house, the water courses, the Dam and every other Convenience to the said mill called Hardie Mill, with the hammer, chisels and crow and all the utensils belonging to the said mill, with half the Millgate and the privilege of going to the Mill Dam with a Cart. Also the garden before the new house.
Also, the said Elizabeth Walch to draw on the 25th of March six pence off James Rothwell yearly and every year on account of the Loom House built by the said James Rothwell on the said dam, also the land from the mill door to the Horsingstone with the Horsingstone, and that it be kept standing and the hedge before the mill. Also the said Elizabeth Walch to pay to her sister Alice, the wife of James Ormrod the sum of 20 shillings yearly and every year on the 25th of March.
I also give and bequeath to my daughter Alice the two old houses, the gardens and shippon at the end of the old house, also the Longshut, Ralph Meadow, Clover Hillock and Hardier Carr, also liberty to all the said ground out of the Mill dam yearly and every year in the month of June. Also the said Alice Ormrod is to pay on Whitsunday seven pounds to the trustees of Bolton Church yearly and every year with all other taxes, lays or other expenses to which the said ground is or may be subject to.
It is also my Will and request and I do give and bequeath to my daughter Ann, the wife of Dennis Kirkman, the New House, the Kitchen, the hearth grate under the Chimney and the Hedge before the Door, also the liberty of going to the dam for water as convenient.
This being the division I have made of my estate to my three daughters, my will and request is that they do quietly and in a friendly manner submit thereto, for should any of my daughters oppose this my last Will by going to law or troubling my Executors in the execution of this my Will, I do hereby declare that such daughter so doing shall be excluded from all their share and shall receive no more than one shilling, and I do order that their share so forfeited shall be paid to the children of that daughter whose share shall be thus forfeited.'

'Executors: John Walch James Ormrod'

'Witness: James Roscoe John Roscoe Abraham Monfreulle'

Little is known about the loomhouse built on the mill dam by James Rothwell as mentioned in the Will. An agreement was made between David Heaton and John Rothwell in 1762 but no further reference has been noted in any documents. The *'Horsingstones'* in front of the mill were a stack of four disused millstones used for mounting horses (A8) which, as mentioned earlier, are now deposited in the rear garden of Bungalow No 83 Hardy Mill Road.

David and Margaret Heaton were worshippers at Cockey New Chapel, otherwise known as the *'Dissenting Chapel of Cockey Moor'*, and now Ainsworth Presbyterian (Unitarian) Chapel. All the daughters were married at Bolton Parish Church, the Chapel not being authorized to conduct marriages in those days. David and Margaret were interred in the Chapel and a brass plate on a pew in the north aisle reads: *'Here resteth the body of Margaret Heaton, the wife of David Heaton of Harwood who departed this life September 19th, 1770 in the 67th year of her age. Also David Heaton who died September 20th, 1784 in the 75th year of his age.'*

To summarize the bequests in David's Will: youngest daughter Ann and Dennis Kirkman were left the new house, Rose Cottage: daughter Alice and James Ormrod were left the two old cottages, the shippon and the four closes of land (ground rent £7 pa): eldest daughter Elizabeth and John Walch were left the mill the adjoining Heaton's Cottage (£1 pa to Alice Ormrod) and the garden before Rose Cottage.

Figure 16 Rose Cottage 1952

Chapter IX THE WALCHS

Branches of the Walch family had been established in Harwood, Cockey Moor and other surrounding districts since the mid-1500s and were associated with Dunscar Fold Farm, Kenyon Farm, Turton, Longsight Farm, Harwood, Walch Fold Farm, Bradshaw and Cox Green Quarry. The spelling of the name varied between Walch, Welch and Walsh over the years, sometimes even between members of the same family, but the form as used in the various documents will be followed in this book.

Robert Walch came from Cockey Moor and in 1720 married Elizabeth Hardman at Radcliffe Parish Church. Between 1722 and 1738 the couple had four children, Ellen, Ellis, John and Joseph. The second son John married Betty Heaton. Robert died in 1765 aged 68 and Elizabeth in 1778 aged 78.

By the time John Walch (1737-1823) and his wife Betty inherited the cornmill in 1784 he was 47 years of age and had probably worked the mill for many years. The extent of their holdings were now confined to the mill, the dam with water courses, the kiln, the coal house, Heaton's Cottage and the garden before Rose Cottage. Two of their three children, Margaret and Samuel were married in 1790 but David was to remain a bachelor.

Margaret married William Thweat (1773-1843), whitster and son of John Thweat who had started Lee Gate Bleachworks in 1782, William and brother James eventually took over the business along with Bridge End Bleachworks located just north of Bradshaw Bridge. Due to financial difficulties in the early 1800s, Lee Gate Works was sold to Ramwell and Pilling, Bridge End Works to Wood and Bentley. By 1834 the Hardcastles of Bradshaw Hall had acquired both businesses (RI9) thus securing the rights of the large watershed of Riding Gate Brook which fed Lee Gate Works. For many years the basement of the Lee Gate premises was used by Lawrence Horrocks and others as a smithy and in 1885 the upper floor was taken over by the Bradshaw, Harwood and Turton Lower End Conservative Association for use as a meeting room and social club.

Samuel left home at the age of 19 to live in Turton but within twelve months he had eloped with Mary Greenhalgh of Walk Mill Farm, Labbys. This *'scandalous'* affair was never forgiven by his father who seemingly had strong puritanical leanings. The situation was made even worse some 25 years later when shortly after Mary's premature death in 1812, Samuel had a forced marriage through childbirth to a Mary Lord.

The story of Samuel and Mary's elopement is best related by Parson Folds, the officiating minister of the marriage and a notable character in the Bolton area at the time (R20).

'Mid way between Bolton and Bradshaw Chapel are sundry old buildings on the slope of the land bordering on the present main road descending to Bradshaw Brook, best known as Labbys. At Labbys dwelt a young female who was the affianced of a young man named Walch from Turton Township. The bridal morn came, but as true love is said never to run smooth, this young Turton Lothario had to receive his bride through the window by stealth as it were with one stocking on, she not having time to pull on the other in order to avoid her parents notice. The parents were opposed to the engagement. "Never mind", said young Walch, "I'll take you with one". The way then to Bolton was by a circuitous route, by the lower ground where Bradshaw Brook flows. The brook had to be forded on tripping stones and before the eager couple could reach Bolton Parish Church, Walch fell from one of these tripping stones and broke his leg. Still undaunted, he insisted on being carried the distance, which he was, and placed at the altar in a kneeling posture (wedding custom). This, however, Parson Folds told Walch he must not do, as he had a newly broken leg, and he sharply and characteristically observed that it was only a Church form'.

In the 1797 Act of Parliament for *'Dividing, Allotting and Inclosing the Commons and Waste grounds within the Township of Harwood'* (R 16) the 302 statute acres of commons which *'in their present State afford very little Benefit to them, but might be considerably improved'*, were allotted to the existing free holders *'in due proportion (Quantity, Quality and Situation considered) to the real Value of their respective Estates'*. Parliament passed some 4000 similar Private and Public Acts between 1750 and 1845 enclosing about 8000 square miles of common land.

In the Enclosure, John Walch was allotted Plot 51 of 2.8 acres and his brother-in-law, James Ormrod was awarded Plot 23 of 2.3 acres. (Figures 17 and 19) John's other brother-in-law, Dyonisious (Dennis) Kirkman was awarded Plot 36 of 0.56 acres adjacent to Longsight, which was eventually the site of Walsh's Institute.

In 1804, Ann Kirkman then a widow and being under the *'necessity of selling'* disposed of Plot 36 to John Walch for 6 guineas. He had paid all the expenses of the Act Commissioners and for the highways and fences and subsequently built a shippon and two cottages on part of the land, a further cottage being added later. It would seem that he also acquired Rose Cottage from Ann about the same time, but no conveyancing deed has been located.

John Walch died in 1823 aged 87 and his Will was proved at Chester the following year (A5). Son David was left all the estate comprising the mill, the kiln, the dam with water courses and Rose Cottage with shippon and outbuildings. He was also left *'Intrust'* Heaton's Cottage in the occupation of John Warburton and the above two cottages on plot 36 in Longsight, which later became known as the *'Institute Cottages'*.

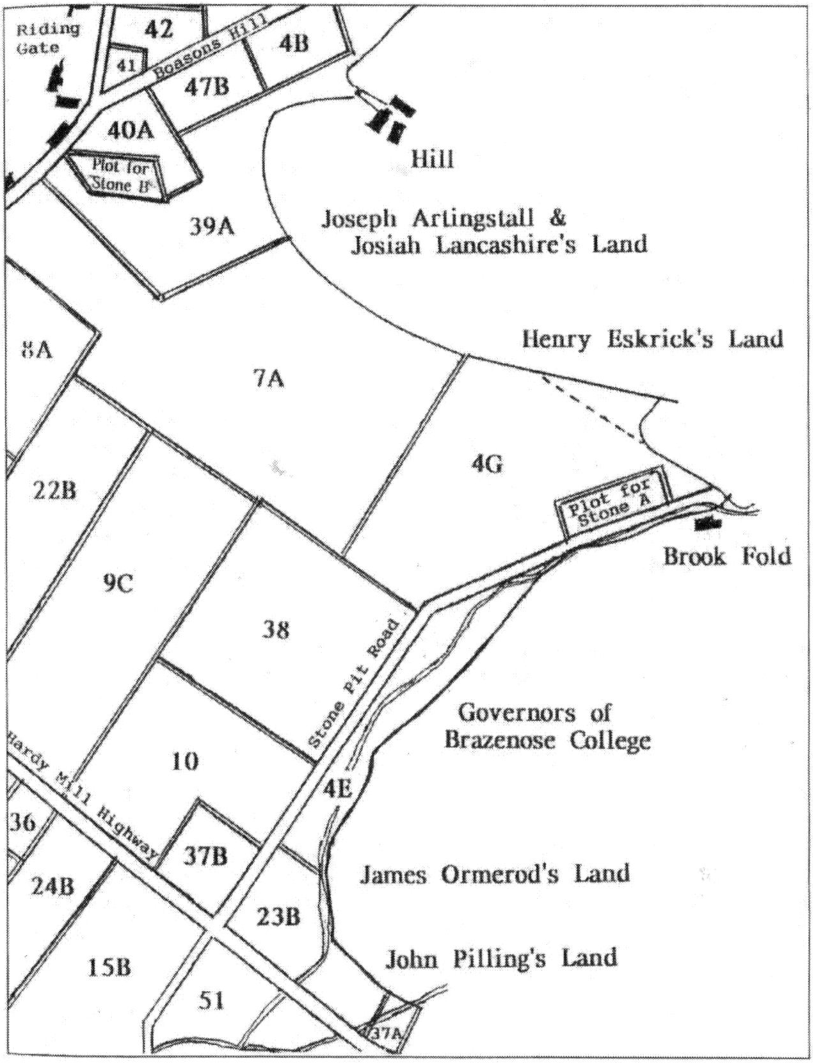

Figure 17 Part Copy of Original Enclosure Plan of 1801.

The rents and profits from these three houses were to be paid to his sister Margaret Thweat for the rest of her natural life, and in her Will of 1830 (A6) she passed on the benefit to her husband William for the rest of his life. David was to receive the first £50 of the rents as a charge for his trusteeship. A ground rent for Heaton's Cottage of £l pa was to be paid to their aunt, Alice Ormrod, her husband James having died in 1801. There was no provision at all in the Will for brother Samuel: the estrangement which had developed with his father after the elopement must have persisted and no doubt been aggravated with his unfortunate second marriage in 1814.

John and Betty Walch were buried at Cockey New Chapel and the monumental inscription reads:- *'This stone is in memory of Betty, the wife of John Walch of Hardy Mill, Harwood who departed this life February 15th, 1803 in the 69th year of her age. Also the aforesaid John Walch who died on the 19th and was here interred on the 22nd day of July, 1823 in the 87th year of his age. Also Margaret, their daughter & wife of William Thweat who died on the 17th and was here interred on the 20th January, 1832 aged 70 years. Also the above named William Thweat who died on the 16th day of January, 1843 aged 70 years. Also David Walch of Hardy Mill, Harwood died 20th of March, 1847 aged 84 years'.* John's parents, Robert and Betty, were buried in an adjacent plot. It seems that Samuel, who died in 1844, was prohibited even from the family grave.

David Walch (1763-1847) had reached the age of 27 when his parents inherited the cornmill in 1790 and had no doubt been working at the mill since his early teens, or before. When he eventually took over from his father he unknowingly became the last miller of Harwood.

Chapter X TROUBLED TIMES

Harwood in the early 1800s was still mainly agricultural and the number of farmsteads had trebled to an estimated thirty-eight over two centuries. Hardy Cornmill, although now mainly trading in processed meal, was still grinding corn by millstone and water power. There were about 2000 water corn mills still operating throughout Great Britain in 1800 but steam power was gradually being introduced into the larger mills.

The first National Census of 1801 registered that the population of the township had increased to nearly 2000. Most of the inhabitants were engaged in the cottage based industries of handloom weaving and spinning but generally with a second occupation such as quarrying, coal mining, bleaching, market-gardening, etc to make a moderate living.

The development of water and steam powered spinning and weaving in the latter half of the 1700s and the introduction of the factory system meant that the cottage operatives were unable to compete with their products. This situation created great hardship and local hostility against the mill-owners flared in 1812 when Bolton handloom weavers burned down the cotton mill of Royce and Dunscough at Westhoughton. Three men and a boy were subsequently hanged for these exploits.

In 1838 James Lee of Brookfold Lane logged in his diary (R21) *'Welts and Satins was 1s.2d in 1836, 5d per yard in 1838. In 1802 at Longsight there were 42 pair of looms going, in 1838 only 7 pairs'.* Other entries in his diary read: *'1826 - Power looms broken at Ramsbottom. Ten men and one woman killed. 1829 - Mill Hill factory was burnt. 1829 - Manchester Riot, 400 power looms burnt'.*

An article in the Bolton Journal of May 1923 observed: *'In 1834, out of a total of 484 families in Harwood, 334 were engaged in hand spinning and hand loom weaving. Out of a total population of 2011 there were 1407 persons busy preparing yarn for the loom and weaving cloth'.* It was not until the strife had subsided in 1845 that power looms were introduced into Harwood when Zachariah Nuttall (A7) started his little water powered weaving shed at the side of Folly Brook in David Walch's Allotment 51 known as Crank's Field.

The main effect of the troubles on Harwood Township was the emigration between 1826 and 1836 of over sixty younger men and women trying to find a new life in America. They sailed from Liverpool to New York which in the days of sail could take up to six weeks. The long journey would no doubt be made somewhat easier with the opening of the Bolton, Bury and Manchester Canal in 1796, and George Stephenson's Bolton to Leigh Railway in 1828 and Manchester to Liverpool Railway in 1830.

Amongst the emigrants to America were six members of the Pilling family from Hardy Mill Farm across the way from the corn mill. Their departure commenced in 1830 with Samuel followed by his brother Ralph who both settled in Philadelphia. Their wives, Sophia and Mary along with sister Mary joined them shortly afterwards as did brother Thomas a couple of years later. In 1851, Ralph died aboard the steamship *'City of Glasgow'* whilst returning from Philadelphia and was buried at Bradshaw Chapel.

John Pilling, (1760-1838) who originated from the Tottington area, had established Hardy Mill Farm in the early 1780s and over the next couple of decades he and his wife Agnes raised a family of five sons and six daughters. By an Indenture of 1795 he had purchased the two cottages, the shippon and two of the closes of land to the north of Hardy Mill Road inherited by Alice and James Ormrod in 1784.

John Pilling seems to have been beset with financial difficulties for most of his days and even in the Enclosures of 1801 when he was allotted Plot 37A & B of total area 1.6 acres (Figures 17 and 19) the award was registered with John Pilling's Mortgagees who were the Haworth family from Tottington. In his Will of September, 1821, as was normal with large families, he left all his estate in trust to his son-in-law John Ramsbottom of Harwood, Yeoman and Thomas Scowcroft of Bradshaw, Coal Merchant (see page 58). The estate included four messuages and parcels of land in the possession of John Walch, James Thomasson, Thomas Haworth, James Haslam and Mary Crompton.

The Will stipulated that any of his children who resided abroad and did not make an appearance in England to receive their share of the residue of the estate (after discharge of the mortgages) within three years of administration, then their share would be divided amongst the children residing in England. This condition was obviously directed at the family emigrants.

The Haworth family were seemingly being very helpful to the Pillings with the mortgages, but to protect their own family interests, several clauses were included in the Will directing the trustees on the disposal of the hereditaments. Edmund Haworth with son John and daughter Mary were the three witnesses. An affidavit filed by Thomas Scowcroft read:

'The 4th of June, 1838. Thomas Scowcroft Executor in this Will named was sworn in common form (John Ramsbottom the other Executor being dead) and he further made oath that the personal estate and effects of the Testator at the time of his death were under the value of £20 before me. J Slade Surrogate (The Testator died 22nd February, 1838). Probate issued. Dated 18th June, 1838. Pending Inhibition'.

Figure 18 Hardy Mill Farm (on the right) c1910.

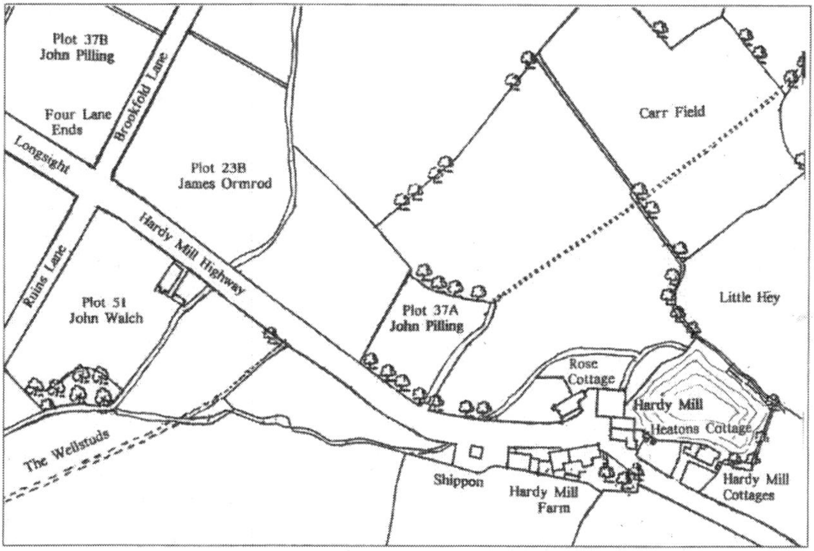

Figure 19 Map of Harwood c1825, showing Enclosure Awards in Hardy Mill Area.

The signatory to the affidavit was Canon James Slade, Vicar of Bolton, Surrogate for the Bishop of Chester. John Pilling was interred at Bradshaw Chapel as was his wife Agnes seven years later.

Shortly after the death of John Pilling, Plot 37B on the corner of Longsight and Brookfold Lane was disposed of as directed by the mortgagees and developed with the cottages on Brookfold Lane, Kay Fields and Tea Company Row, numbers 191 to 205 Longsight (A4). The Black Cock beer house (or jerry shop) was built on the corner (Figure 20) and opened by John Greenhalgh (Black Jack) in 1860. He was the publican until his death in 1881, his wife Alice having died a year earlier.

Soon afterwards Edmund Holden, who had recently vacated Longsight Farm, took over and occupied the beerhouse with his wife Ann and their three children. Then followed landlords John Booth and Patrick Riley, and the last publican in 1896 was Richard Atkinson. After two years he turned the public house into a butchers shop and added a slaughter house at the rear. Ten years later the Atkinsons moved further down the road to No 54 Longsight where they remain today as family butchers (see rear cover).

Figure 20 Former location of the Black Cock Inn. The end of Tea Company Row is on the left.

Chapter XI THE LAST MILLER

When David Walch inherited the Hardy Mill Estate in 1823 he lived at Rose Cottage and three years later he purchased the large triangular piece of land behind the house which he used as a garden. This was formerly part of a close of land called the Calliate or Croft owned by John Pilling and David paid £10 for the plot to John and his mortgagees, the Haworths. It is interesting to note that Samuel Walch, who was still working Walk Mill Farm over at Labbys (Figure 21), was a fifth party to the Indenture of this conveyance, so it was apparent that the two brothers were still in contact regardless of the family differences.

On Christmas Day 1836, James Lee logged in his diary (R21): *'One load of meal stolen from Hardy Mill'.* In 1910, Samuel Scowcroft added the comment: *'A corn mill was here where the oats was made into meal. The last person in charge was John Whittle. He worked for Charles Hopwood who was occupier. The grinding was done by water power from the mill dam which is now filled up. As a little boy I remember being shewn the kiln on which the oats were'.*

David lost his sight in 1839 at the age of 76. John Whittle (1795-1867) had been his assistant at the mill for many years and, as noted by Samuel Scowcroft, carried on running the corn merchanting business after David's death in 1847. As previously mentioned, David was buried in the family grave at Cockey Moor Chapel. His Will of 1845 was very concise and self explanatory and is presented here in full.

Figure 21 Walk Mill Farm, Labbys.
Photograph taken in 1910 showing 'Shaky Bridge'. over Bradshaw Brook.

'I David Walch of Hardy Mill in the Township of Harwood in the Parish of Bolton-le-Moors and County Palatine of Lancaster, Miller, do declare and publish this as my last Will and Testament hereby revoking and annulling all former Wills and Testaments made by me. After the payment of my lawful and just debts and funeral expenses, I give and bequeath all my property of every description whether consisting in real or personal estate to my esteemed friend Charles James Darbishire Esq, of the Folds, Little Bolton. And I hereby appoint the Reverend James Whitehead of Broomfield, Ainsworth, Minister of the Gospel and John Dean Esq of Silverwell House, Great Bolton, Executors of this my last Will with power to either or both of them in case of death or resignation to appoint others in their place and stead, Signed by me this Seventh day of May, 1845.'
'DAVID WALCH Signed by me said David Walch as and for his last Will and Testament in the presence of us and of each other'.

'JAMES KIRKMAN -JOHN WHITTLE'

'In the Consistory Court of Chester - the Sixteenth day of November, 1847. Appeared personally John Whittle of Harwood in the County of Lancaster, Miller, and being sworn upon the gospel made Oath that he is one of the attesting witnesses to the last Will and Testament of David Walch late of Hardy Mill in the Parish of Bolton-le-Moors in the County of Lancaster, Miller deceased, bearing date the Seventh day of May, 1845 and hereto annexed that he was present on the said Seventh day of May and saw the said David Walch, deceased, duly execute the same as & for his last Will and Testament by signing his name David Walch at the foot or end thereof as it now appears. James Kirkman the other attesting witness being also present at the same time Deponent and the said James Kirkman did then in the presence of the said Testator and of each other sit and subscribe their names thereto as witnesses as they now appear. JOHN WHITTLE - Sworn at Bolton the day & year aforesaid before me. J Slade Surrogate'

The above affidavit filed by John Whittle would be necessary due to David Walch's loss of sight. The signatory was Canon James Slade, Vicar of Bolton. The Rev James Whitehead was the minister at Cockey New Chapel and John Dean was a cotton merchant. The following notice was published in the Bolton Chronicle on August 19th, 1848.

'Hardy Mill, Harwood, near Bolton To be let for a term of years'.
'The above convenient & long-established Corn Mill late in the possession of Mr David Walch deceased. With the mill will be let an excellent dwelling house & garden of which immediate possession may be had; and at some future time, if required, about four statute acres of excellent land may be added to the occupancy. Reply to John Dean, Esq, Silverwell House, Bolton or to the Rev J Whitehead, Broomfield, Ainsworth'.

Chapter XII THE HOPWOODS

Charles Hopwood (1806-1874) with his wife Ellen and family arrived in the district from Horwich about 1838 and purchased Hardy Mill Farm and estate from the Executors of John Pilling. There were several families of Hopwood in Horwich at the time, and Charles was the elder of the five children of John and Magdalene Hopwood. Within a couple of years of their arrival his wife Ellen prematurely died in 1841 at the age of 31, seemingly on the birth of their fifth son Alexander. She was buried in her native township of Horwich at Holy Trinity Church, as were her husband's family and her third son, Charles, who died 27 years later, also at 31 years of age.

As well as working the farm, Charles started to operate the quarry up Brookfold Lane and the Land Tax Returns of 1845 record Hopwood and Haslam's Stone Delph with a rateable value of £33-5s. Partner Haslam was most likely John Haslam who at the time was living in the community with his *'tally wife'* Mary Booth.

The redundant corn mill was later rented from the Executors of David Walch and converted into a stone mason's yard, working the stone from the quarry and using the waterwheel to drive the stone-cutting and shaping machinery. Stone from the yard was used to build Harwood Wesleyan Chapel on Longsight in 1862 and no doubt many other buildings in the locality. Dressed stones (and even a stone lavatory basin) were still scattered about the premises 100 years later.

Figure 22 Harwood Wesleyan Chapel,built in 1862 with stone from Hopwood's Quarry.

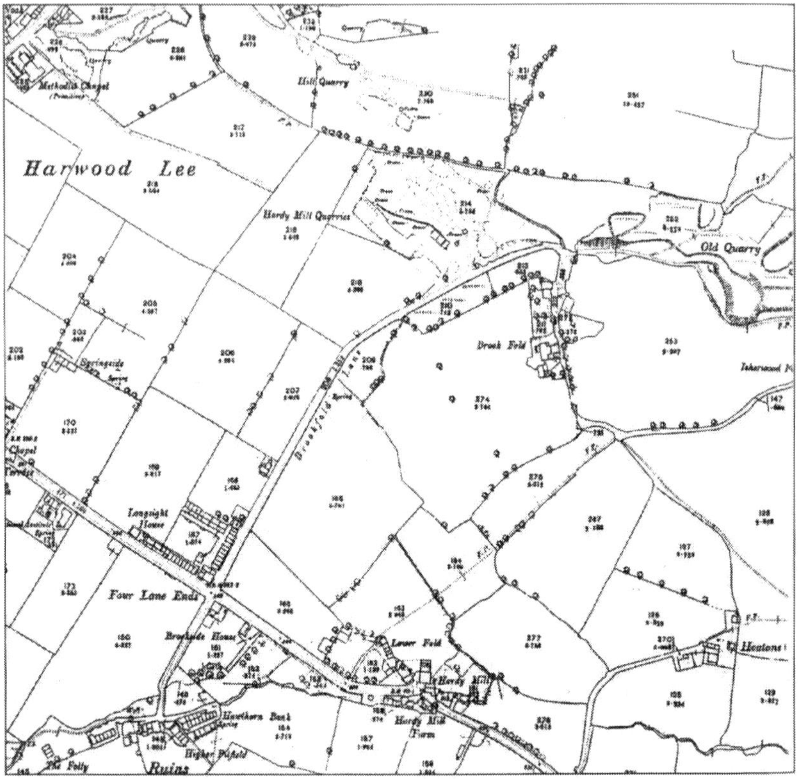

Figure 23 Plan of Brookfold Lane Area, Harwood 1890.

In the Enclosures of 1801, Plots A&B each of ½ acre, were designated adjacent to Stone Pit Road (now Brookfold Lane) and Tottington Road for quarrying *'sand, stone and gravel to repair the public roads and ways within the township of Harwood'* (Figure 17). Charles Hopwood's quarry was an extension of Plot A into Plot 4G which had been awarded to the Governors of Brazenose College.

Charles leased a plot of land off Stone Pit Road for two periods of 21 years starting 1851 from the Rev James Slade of Bolton Parish Church. This had been Plot 38 of 6.1 statute acres awarded to the Curate of Little Lever Chapel in the Enclosures. He also took a lease on Brookfold Farm and acquired the remainder of the land held by the Ormrods (with ground rent of £7) probably via his second wife of 1851, Alice Ormrod, the great grand-daughter of James Ormrod. A further acquisition was Heaton's Cottage purchased from David Walch's legatee, Charles Darbishire cl850 (see next chapter).

The sixth National Census of 1851 provided more details of the householders and not only recorded the name, age and occupation of each individual, but also the birthplace, relationship and marital status. It is interesting to examine the 1851 Census Returns for Harwood which show a cross section of local working families at that time in the early days of the Victorian Era. The accommodation of the Hardy Mill community had been increased about 1840 with the building of the five cottages of Lower Fold.

Charles Hopwood, widower, was the Quarry Master employing 31 men. He was also farming 50 acres at Hardy Mill Farm helped by his two elder sons Hugh and John, and probably others. His three youngest sons, Charles, Robert and Alexander were scholars and Mary Smith from Westhoughton was the servant.

In the various cottages were George Holt from Tottington with Susana and 3 children, Benjamin Greenhalgh with Ann and 4 children and John Whittle (erstwhile miller) with Catherine and 5 children, all the men being farm workers probably at Hardy Mill Farm. Other families were Edward Farnworth from Blackrod with Alise and 5 children, John Haslam with *'tally wife'* Mary Booth and her 4 children, William Lowe from Coppull with Alise and 4 children and John Greenhalgh with Mary and son. The men were entered as block-cutter, stone-mason, carter and painter, most likely all working at the quarry. Finally, John Allen with Martha and 6 children and James Allen with Esther and son were handloom weavers and Thomas Ingham from Walton-le-Dale with wife Isabela was a cotton printer.

The eleven households included a total of thirty seven children and, whilst some of the families had migrated from outlying districts, others had lived and worked in the Hardy Mill community for many years. The Hopwoods, Whittles and Booths were all residents for thirty years or more, during which time some of the men had changed occupations.

Figure 24 Lower Fold 1975. Built about 1840, apparently in two phases.

Charles Hopwood must have very quickly made an impact after his arrival in the township for in 1844 he was elected Guardian (of the poor) for Harwood, a post he held for the rest of his life. In 1865 he was appointed Chairman of the Bolton Board of Guardians and in the same year laid the corner stone of the Poor Law Offices on Mawdsley Street. He held the office for eight years and is named on a plaque in the entrance to the Fishpool Workhouse (now part of the Royal Bolton Hospital) recording the opening in 1861.

He died in October, 1874 aged 68 and his Will was proved at Manchester two months later. He left his estate in trust to his sons Hugh, John and Alexander requesting that they carry on the businesses of Farmer, Quarry Owner and Stone Dealer until the expiration of the leases on the farm and quarry. To manage the concerns, Hugh was to be paid £l-10s per week and John £1-5s per week. Whenever the businesses were terminated, all the assets and capital investment were to be divided five ways between the four surviving sons and the two children of the late Charles. Charles Hopwood was interred at Christ's Church and his second wife Alice, who died ten years later, was interred at St Maxentius Church with her parents.

None of the Hopwood sons lived to a great age. The first son, Hugh, occupied Rose Cottage and carried on managing the farm and quarry until his death in 1878 at the age of 46 when his wife Mary and her three daughters moved to Brook Fold Farm.

John, the second son survived the longest of the family and died at Ox Shut Gate Farm in 1897 aged 62; he never quite attained the position of Guardian, losing the election in 1884 by 3 votes to John Scowcroft from Springside Farm. The middle son Charles died in Manchester at the early age of 31 and as mentioned earlier, was buried near his mother at Holy Trinity Church, Horwich. The youngest son, Alexander, died in 1876 at the age of 35.

Robert, the fourth son, ran a blacksmith and wheelwright business at Hardy Mill from about 1860 and the rear extension to the premises and chimney were no doubt added later to accommodate the necessary furnaces and equipment. The waterwheel would be used to drive the bellows and machinery. Robert died in 1876 at the age of 38.

Figure 25 Hardy Mill c1940 showing rear extension and chimney (also rear of Rose Cottage and Lower Fold).

Chapter. XIII DAVID WALSH'S CHARITY

In his Will of 1845, David Walch left to his *'esteemed friend Charles James Darbishire'* all his real and personal estate in trust, with the intention of establishing a Charity Trusteeship. Charles Darbishire was a notable civic dignitary of Bolton, and had been a partner in the cotton manufacturing concern of John Heywood and Son from 1822 to 1842: he was also Secretary of the Bolton Mechanics Institute for about the same period. When Bolton was granted a Borough Charter under the Act of 1838 (2nd in England), Great and Little Bolton were incorporated into Bolton Borough and Charles Darbishire was elected the first Mayor by the new council. He gave his name to Darbishire Park near Waterloo Street for which he donated the land in 1868. Charles died at Vale Bank, Rivington in 1874 aged 76.

It was twenty years before the charity trusteeship was finally set up and the preamble to the Trust Deed of 1865 is shown in Figure 26, A fully detailed description of the hereditaments follows in the Indenture, which is summarised below, and the Plan Referred To is shown in Figure 27.

1	Three cottages and gardens (Institute Cottages, Figure 28)
2	Meadow (Site of Walsh's Institute)
3	Cottage and garden (Brookside House, 10 Hardy Mill Rd)
4	Meadow
5	Meadow, plantation and brook
6	Pasture
7	Shippon & Waste
8	Garden (behind farm)
9	Rose Cottage and gardens (in the occupation of Charles Hopwood)
10	Mill, kiln and dam (in the occupation of Charles Hopwood)

One of the cottages held *'intrust'* by David Walch was Heaton's Cottage which is omitted from the above list of hereditaments. As mentioned earlier, the cottage had previously been sold by Charles Darbishire to Charles Hopwood but a deed for this conveyance has not been located. The purchase price of the cottage along with the accrued rents would be included in the £700 paid over to the Trust.

The first Annual Meeting of the Trustees of David Walsh's Charity (Walch was changed to Walsh in the Trust Deed) was held in the vestry of Bank Street Chapel, Bolton in January, 1867. This was to be the regular venue for annual meetings of the trust for the next 50 years. Two years later the Treasurer reported that the balance in hand at the bank of Hardcastle, Cross & Company was £l091-16s-4d and the total annual rents from the property and land of the estate was £47-4s.

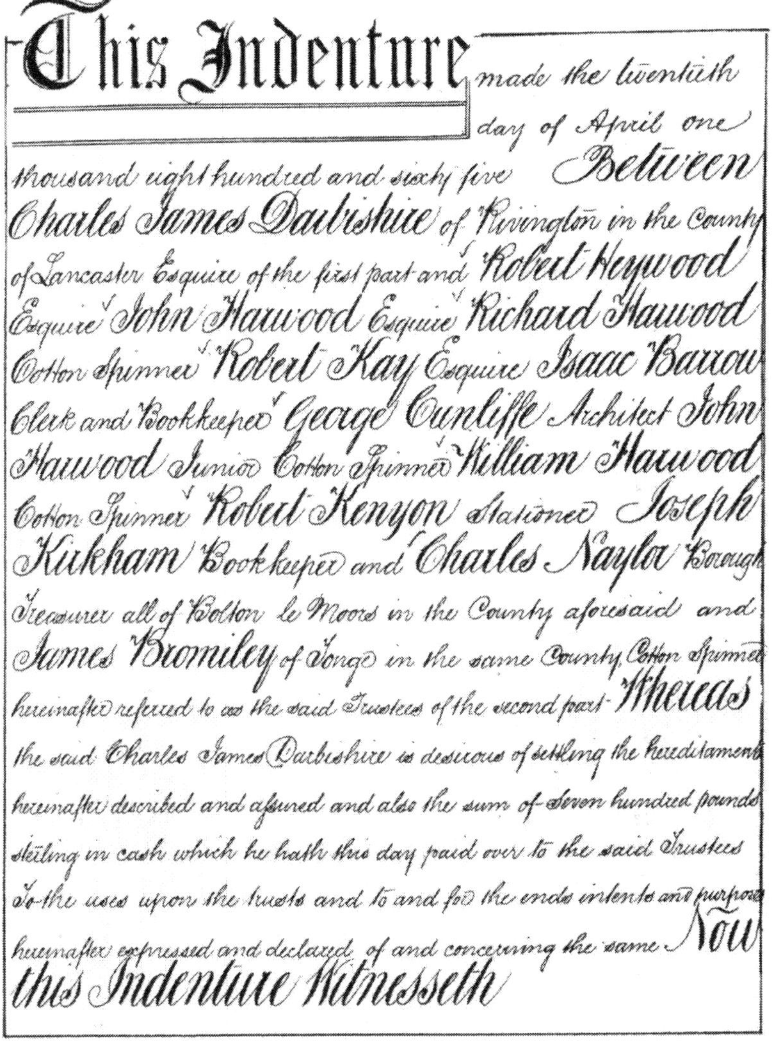

This Indenture made the twentieth day of April one thousand eight hundred and sixty five Between Charles James Darbishire of Rivington in the County of Lancaster Esquire of the first part and Robert Heywood Esquire John Harwood Esquire Richard Harwood Cotton Spinner Robert Kay Esquire Isaac Barrow Clerk and Bookkeeper George Cunliffe Architect John Harwood Junior Cotton Spinner William Harwood Cotton Spinner Robert Kenyon Stationer Joseph Kirkham Bookkeeper and Charles Naylor Borough Treasurer all of Bolton le Moors in the County aforesaid and James Bromiley of Tonge in the same County Cotton Spinner hereinafter referred to as the said Trustees of the second part Whereas the said Charles James Darbishire is desirous of settling the hereditaments hereinafter described and assured and also the sum of seven hundred pounds sterling in cash which he hath this day paid over to the said Trustees To the uses upon the trusts and to and for the ends intents and purposes hereinafter expressed and declared of and concerning the same Now this Indenture Witnesseth

Figure 26 Preamble to the Trust Deed.

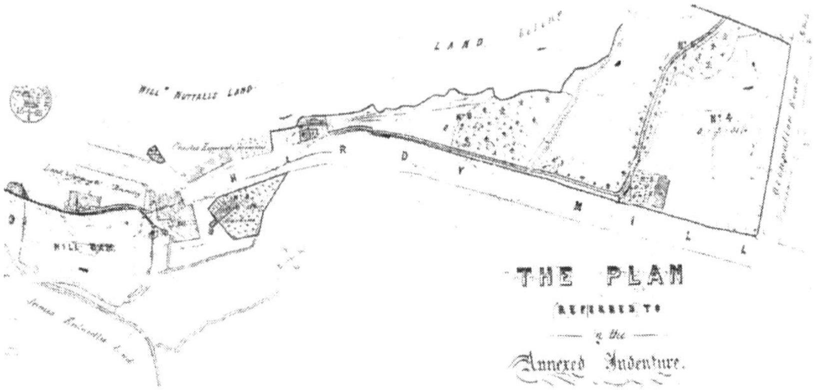

Figure 27 Plan Referred to in Trust Deed of 1865.

Figure 28 Institute Cottages, Longsight demolished in 1974. Used by the Harwood Wesleyans from 1818 until their Chapel School was built in 1822 and known as '*Prayer House Cottages*'.

Figure 29 Brookside House 10 Hardy Mill Road, used as Tea Rooms and Shop before 1959.

Figure 30 Christ's Church School in 1933, built in 1848.

There is no suggestion in David Walch's Will of providing a school but the Trust Deed lays down *'That the Trustees should erect a Building for use as a School or Schools, Public Library and Reading Room for the general education, instruction and rational amusement of the inhabitants of the Township of Harwood and the neighbourhood thereof'*

By 1870, plans for a new institute building had been prepared by the architects, Cunliffe and Truman of Bolton, and a year later a tender of £900 for construction of the building was accepted from J & J Leach. The site was to be the plot on Longsight purchased by John Walch in 1804 from Ann Kirkman. The building was to be *'designated Walsh's Educational Institute and the date of its erection be placed thereon'.*

Construction was complete by 1872 and on the day of the opening, Saturday May 4th, tea was served to about 150 people at 5.00 pm. The proceedings were opened at 6.00 pm by the Chairman, John Harwood JP, and entertainment was provided later by several singers and the choir of Bank Street Chapel. Admission was eight pence and new members were enrolled during the evening.

Two church schools had already been established in the locality catering for the basic elementary education of the children. The first, Harwood Wesleyan Chapel/School, was built on Longsight in 1822. Later, after the opening of Christ's Church in 1840, a small school was founded in a cottage near Lomax Fold, but in 1848 a new school to accommodate about 150 pupils was built further down Stitch-mi-Lane.

The first Government involvement in elementary education was in 1833 when 50% grants were offered to religious bodies and other organisations towards the cost of new schools. The Education Act of 1870 initiated free schooling and payment of teachers by the local authority and in 1880 attendance became compulsory for children of 5 to 13 years of age.

In the early days of the Institute, the main usage of the premises was as a members' library and reading rooms, with Elementary Evening Classes on the upper floor. It was also a popular venue for meetings of political parties, Local Authority Departments, the Mechanics Institute and other bodies. In 1874, the Harwood Township Meeting was held at the Institute in an attempt to move these meetings away from the public houses, but this was the one and only occasion.

The new Institute actually acted as a day school for eight months in 1880 when the scholars from Harwood Wesleyan School occupied the premises at *'a rate of 20 shillings per calendar month, they to pay also the cost of lighting, warming and cleaning the premises'.* This was whilst their new school was under construction on the site of the old Chapel. (Figure 32).

Figure 31 Old Wesleyan Chapel/School
Built in 1822 on present site of Longsight Methodist Church Hall.

Figure 32 Sketch of Harwood Wesleyan Chapel and School.
The chapel was built in 1862, the School was built in 1880 and demolished in 1958.

The premises were *'modernised'* in 1920 with the installation of electric lighting, and in 1928 the Lancashire County Council Elementary Education Committee leased the upper floor for Handicraft Classes for children attending other schools in the district. The Institute was also used as a Child Welfare Centre for a period and as an Air Raid Wardens Post during World War ll. From 1939, the Lancashire County Council Library Committee utilised part of the building as a Public Library until the new Harwood Library was opened in 1969.

The Institute with its central position in the area has been a great amenity to the township over the years and recently its usage has increased to almost full capacity. At the time of writing, the upper floor is taken up on weekdays with the *'Kids Core'* and on Sundays the lower floor is used both morning and afternoon by the Trinity Presbyterians and Harwood Christadelphians. Throughout the week there are classes in arts and crafts such as drama, dancing, painting, ceramics, flower arranging and needle craft, and for the more nimble are activities such as yoga, weight watching and line-dancing. Even the dog lovers are catered for with a training and handling course for their pets.

Figure 33 Walsh's Educational Institute.

Chapter XIV HEATON'S FARM

When John Kirkman (c1700-1764) acquired Heatons Farm in 1745, he already held leases on estates in Ainsworth and Openshaw, Manchester. He had married Esther Allen of Radcliffe in 1721 and they had two sons, Zachariah and Robert, and a daughter Alice. It would appear that generally John and his eldest son Zachariah ran the Ainsworth and Heatons estates and younger son Robert operated the estate at Openshaw. John Kirkman made his Will in 1759 nominating his wife Esther and sons Zachariah and Robert as Executors, but before the Will was proved at Chester in 1764, Esther had died. This left the two sons with the three estates, but with provisos for various payments to be made from the profits and rents to daughter Alice Farnworth, and also Martha Valentine and Mary Brady who were probably faithful servants of the family.

He bequeathed to Zachariah the messuage, land and premises by the name of Heatons and also the Right of Title and Interest in the land and tenement at Ainsworth held in lease under Ralph Ashton of Middleton. Robert inherited the land, tenement and premises at Openshaw held by lease under Leigh of Higher Leigh.

Zachariah sold all the 22 acres of land at Heatons to William Kennedy of Manchester in 1782 and there then followed a complex series of conveyances and mortgages on the estate involving amongst others, Ann Crompton of Bolton, Thomas Nuttall of Little Bolton, Thomas Taylor, Solicitor of Bolton, Thomas Henry Monk, Tallow Merchant of Bolton and the Governors of Bolton Grammar School.

Zachariah's son John, however, retained a part ownership of the property until about 1820 and in the Enclosures of 1801, he was awarded Plot 10 of 5.2 acres surrounding John Pilling's Block 13B (see Figures 17 & 19) on the corner of Hardy Mill Highway and Stone Pit Road. (later Longsight and Brookfold Lane) This plot was eventually the site of St Brendan's School and playground. On the Enclosure Map, the entrance to Heaton's Farm from Hardy Mill Road was designated Kirkman's Gate.

From about 1780, the tenancy of the Heatons Estate was held by the Entwistle family from Lostock and they operated the farm for the next 80 years or so starting with Richard and later Cataran. The last of the family to work the farm was James who, with his wife Ann and family, occupied the premises from about 1840. Two years after James's death in 1860, his son and daughter, William and Esther, moved from Heatons to Longsight House which they had built on John Kirkman's Plot 10. William lived to the great age of 90 and was interred at St Maxentius Church, Bradshaw, as were most of the Entwistle family.

Chapter XV   JOSHUA LOMAX

The object of Joshua Lomax in returning to Harwood shortly before his death in 1685/6 as mentioned in Chapter Vll was to purchase Heaton's Estate and settle an endowment on Bolton Parish Church.

Joshua was born at Breightmet Fold, Bolton in 1625 and educated at Bolton School *'in his time most famous for learning'*. He was the grandson of James Lomax of Oakenbottom and an ancestor of Robert Lomax of Harwood, founder of Christ's Church. In 1645 Joshua and John Lomax of Harwood sold land to Richard Goodwin, one time Vicar of Bolton, when Joshua was noted as being of St Albans. He must have moved from Bolton about this time for some unknown reason (Civil War?). He had four children with his wife Anne; Joshua, Thomas, Mary and John.

From 1650 onward he was involved in numerous conveyances in the St Alban's area, his two main acquisitions being the manor of Childwickbury, held by the family from 1666 to 1854, and the manor of Westbrook Hey, held from 1667 to 1779. Son Joshua succeeded to Childwickbury and Thomas to Westbrook Hey. Other properties acquired were Bourne Hall, held from 1656 to 1667 and an estate at Redbourne held briefly 1650/1.

Joshua was appointed Sheriff of Hertfordshire in 1674 and probably assumed Arms at this time: (*'Ermine a running greyhound sable between three scallops gules'*). His first son, Joshua, was MP for St Albans from 1708 to 1721. The second son of Joshua II, Caleb, was MP from 1710 to his death in 1729.

By his Will of December 26th, 1685 (Probate proved 1686), Joshua left endowments to the Parish Church of Bolton and four churches in St Albans. A copy of his Will - 60 pages long - is held at Hertfordshire County Archives, along with 50 or so deeds. An extract from the Will hangs on the west wall of Christ's Church, Harwood.

To the Parish Church of Bolton, St Peters, he charged his messuages, mill and lands in Harwood (Heatons and Hardy Mill) with the yearly rental of £7. One pound of this bequest was for the Vicar of Bolton to preach, morning and afternoon of Whit Sunday yearly, a sermon on the text from Matthew, Chapter 6, Verse 33: *'But seek ye first ye Kingdom of God and His righteousness and all things shall be added unto you'.* Also, forty poor housekeepers in the hamlets of Breightmet and Harwood who brought as many of their family as possible to hear the sermons were to receive sixpence each. He added: *'I heartily pray that some vile wretch may come for the sixpence, and be catched and converted'.* The remainder of the endowment was to subsidize a poor scholar from Bolton School to attend university to be a *'minister of the word of God'.*

In St Albans he charged his lands called Black Cross and other lands in the parish of St Michaels with the yearly payment of £8. Likewise, one pound was for the rector of the Abbey Church to preach two sermons on the same text from Matthew on the Sunday after Easter. Also one shilling each was to be given to 20 poor housekeepers of the parish who attended the church to hear the sermons. Similar grants were endowed to the three other parishes of St Peters, St Michaels and St Stephens, but apparently to be applied on different Sundays around Whitsuntide. He added: *'Perhaps by the goodness of God and assistance of his Spirit co-working with his Word, some vile wretch who lives without God in the world for the lucre of XIId may come to be converted'.*

The vault of the Lomax family is in the churchyard of St Michaels which is adjacent to the Roman site of Verulamium. An inscription around the top of the vault reads: *'Blessed is he that considereth the poor and needy. The Lord shall deliver him in the hour of trouble. Thou Lord art good and gracious and of great mercy with all them that call upon Thee'.* The vault was installed in 1866, as was a window in the church: *'In memoriam patis delecti Joshue Lomax obit'.*

Figure 34 The Lomax Family Vault, St Michaels Church, St Albans

Chapter XVI LATTER DAYS

Towards the end of the 1800s, Harwood was still mainly rural with about 35 farms and little industry. The population had contracted by just under a quarter in the previous 50 years and one in every five of the 320 dwellings in the township was standing empty. Since the decline of the cottage based industries of handloom weaving and spinning, the younger people had moved out of the district to find employment in the cotton mills, bleach crofts and engineering works of Bolton, which at the time were running at a peak

Improvements were in the offing and, despite much resistance from local bodies, statutory services began to be installed in the district. Piped water from Bolton Corporation Waterworks arrived in 1882, as did some street gas lamps. Five years later the main sewer was laid and in 1899 the first electric tram ran from Bolton to the Royal Oak at Bradshaw.

Previous to the arrival in the district of a piped system, the Hardy Mill community had been supplied with water from wells at Heatons and Well Studs and a spout and tub at the Mill. According to a report of 1880 from Bolton District Sanitary Authority, the two wells supplied 14 households and the field drain spout at Hardy Mill supplied 6 houses. Domestic supplies of water from all three sources were considered to be sufficient and of good quality.

In 1881, two children of residents David Greenhalgh and Joseph Snape were drowned in the mill dam and their bodies were removed from the water by another resident, John Holden. Three years later a summons was issued by the Sanitary Authority regarding the nuisance caused by the lodge and over the next decade the dam was filled in.

The kiln building annexed to the mill which had later been used as a workshop, was converted into a cottage in 1882 under the direction of J T Simpson shortly after his appointment as Property Agent for David Walsh's Charity, a post he held for 25 years. It was first occupied by James Holt who had continued the wheelwright business of Robert Hopwood and was the last person to use the waterwheel. He is recorded in 1897 as taking a 14 year lease on the mill, water courses, cottage and garden at a rent of £8 per year. James operated the business until his death in 1906, and both he and his wife Sarah were interred at Christ's Church, Harwood. The residue of his lease on the premises was completed by Arthur Miles and in 1914 Peter Kirkman took a further lease for a term of ten years.

In the mid-1920s, Jack Booth and his wife Emily occupied the property and it came to be known as Booth's Cottage. Jack established a small-holding on the filled in mill lodge with two large greenhouses and specialised in growing begonias and keeping goats. They had a daughter Hilda and son Jack who was an Air Gunner in the RAF and sadly killed in 1944 aged 23. When the Booths departed in 1969, Alf and Barbara Partington purchased the cottage from David Walsh's Charity and have since demolished the greenhouses and restored the property and garden, sensitively retaining as much of the original construction as possible, including the waterwheel.

After the demise of the Hopwoods in 1878, Rose Cottage was occupied by Thomas Walsh Best (1838-1907) from Bolton with his wife Mary Ann and their six children. He took a full repair lease for a term of 21 years on the house, outbuilding and garden at a rent of £8 per annum. Thomas was a master brushmaker and a partner in the firm of Best and Eyland, Brush and Rope Manufacturers, Oxford Street, Bolton of which he was eventually the sole owner. He moved back to Bolton in 1885 and two years later the cottage was leased to Charles Richardson, an upholsterer, at the same rental.

Towards the end of the century, John Thomas Scowcroft (1865-1931) moved into Rose Cottage. He came from Waterloo Street, Bolton and had married Mary Jane Ryder in 1893; they had five children, of which the last three were baptised at Harwood Wesleyan Chapel. He was a member of the extensive Scowcroft family whose pedigree stretches back for more than thirty generations and spans over eight centuries (R22).

It will be sufficient for the purpose of this history to only go back through four generations to John Thomas's great-great-grandfather, William Scowcroft who lived at Brookbottom Farm in the 1700s and was the proprietor of the Raikes Coal Pits on Tottington Road. He was the common ancestor of John Thomas and Jethro Scowcroft who will be referred to later in the chapter.

John Thomas had inherited from his father, John, the business of yeast merchants and importers established by the family in Folds Road, Bolton about 1830, and which was reportedly one of the oldest businesses of its kind in the Bolton District. John very soon transferred part of the retail yeast business to Hardy Mill and in 1907 the company was recorded as John T Scowcroft, Yeast Importers, 1 Hardy Mill. By the 1930s the business had developed into a wholesale yeast merchants operating from both Folds Road and Hardy Mill. John Thomas died in 1954 aged 87 and was interred at Harwood Wesleyan Chapel, as were several other members of this branch of the family.

The original mill building was finally demolished after the roof had collapsed in 1919 and John Scowcroft (1903-1974), the youngest son of John Thomas, converted what was left of the premises into a garage. In 1929 he installed on the forecourt of the building the first electric petrol pumps in Turton district (Figure 35). He eventually sold the business to the Mobil Oil Company who, in 1965, erected a new petrol station in part of the large garden of Rose Cottage.

John retired four years later and moved from Rose Cottage to the bungalow he had recently built a little further down Hardy Mill Road on a plot awarded to John Pilling's Mortgagees in 1801. The old premises were subsequently demolished, the chimney having been felled back in 1945, and a new bungalow built on the site in 1975.

Jethro Scowcroft (1829-1880), from another branch of the family, acquired 4/5ths of Hardy Mill Farm and estate from Charles Hopwood c1870 and eventually took over the lease on Brookfold Lane Quarry. The residual 1/5th of the estate was later purchased by an Indenture of 1902 between the various Executors.

Jethro was the youngest of eleven children and in 1855 had inherited Tonge Colliery and other pits from his father, Thomas, who was the grandson of William Scowcroft of Brookbottom Farm, the common ancestor previously mentioned. The colliery was located on the north side of the River Tonge between Tonge Moor Road and Ainsworth Lane and adjacent to the appropriately named Jethro Street and Scowcroft Street.

Figure 35 Rose Cottage & Hardy Mill Garage with petrol pumps c1965.

Jethro and his wife Margaret lived at Moorfield House, a mansion with 14 acres of land at Tonge Moor, and they had two sons and five daughters. In his Will of 1880, he appointed his wife and brother-in-law Peter Duxbury as trustees until his two sons, Thomas of Bromley Cross and Henry Turner of Breightmet, reached the age of 25. During this period Hardy Mill Farm was worked and occupied by Thomas Higson and later Albert Howarth.

By 1908, James Demosthenes Brooks, an Estate Agent from Farnworth had acquired Hardy Mill Farm, and during that year he purchased Heatons Farm, Heatons Cottage and the two *'old cottages'* with closes of land adjacent to Hardy Mill Road. These were conveyed in three agreements of April, September and December from the Trustees of Jethro Scowcroft, Thomas Henry Monk, and the Governors of Bolton Grammar School at a total cost of £2689-9s-6d. In the latter agreement the £7 ground rent initiated by Joshua Lomax in 1685 was finally extinguished with a freehold reversion by the purchase of consolidated stock of £280 at 2½% interest. This considerable estate was later conveyed to William Russell, a solicitor from Lostock in 1925 and again in 1934 to Wilfred Andrews, a builder from Great Lever who built the semi-detached houses on Hardy Mill Road between Brookfold Lane and Greenwoods Lane.

Figure 36 Hardy Mill in 1931 after the road improvements.

Hardy Mill Farm was tenanted in 1914 by Arnold Hurst and his sisters Evelyn and Florence who used the barn for concerts in winter and tea rooms in summer. The farm buildings were eventually acquired by the Local Authority and demolished when Hardy Mill Road was widened in 1927-30 after a fatal accident at *'Skenning Corner'*, as it was colloquially known (Figure 36). Part of the property was occupied about this time by a niece of the Hursts, Margaret Kay and her husband Julius who had a motorcycle business on Bradshawgate, Bolton.

A popular spot between the wars was Crank's Tea Rooms at Brookside House, 10 Hardy Mill Road. This property had been leased to George Kinnersley in 1909 by David Walsh's Charity but the Crank family later occupied the premises and opened a little cafe and sweetshop. The garden to the cafe had a babbling brook and a see-saw and swings for the children, and also an open fronted *'pavilion'* in which refreshments were served; the roof of this lean-to can still be seen behind the stone wall on Hardy Mill Road. John and Olive Rushton acquired the business after WW2 and, during the fifties operated the cafe and shop selling such specialities as home-made jam, lemon-cheese and new laid eggs. John was a slaughterman and Olive ran the teashop until it closed shortly before 1959 when the property was acquired by Jim and Florence Mather.

After the departure of the Entwistles in 1862, Heaton's Farm was tenanted by Ralph Whittle and then in 1876 by James Green Howarth from Heaton. Towards the end of the century the tenancy was taken by James Lambert, a stone-mason who also owned Uglow Quarry in Broadhead Valley near Edgworth. His daughter married a cotton spinner called Greenwood and she ran the farm with her brother James, with whom she had previously rented and worked Dewhurst Farm. The Greenwoods had two children, a daughter Helen and son Stanley Lambert who eventually took over the farm; he purchased the estate from Wilfred Andrews in 1940 and operated the farm and milk round until his retirement in 1975.

In October, 1995, Stanley related to the writer his memories of the floods in Harwood and Bradshaw of August, 1927. Torrential rain on the slopes above Heatons Farm swelled and scoured out the course of the brook and flooded Hardy Mill, demolishing an internal wall in Booths Cottage and sweeping an old-type mangle down to Brookfold Lane. Stanley vividly recalled how he had helped to remove some flagstones to release the deluge of water into the old mill-race and avoid further destruction. He died in January 1996 aged 88.

Whilst the rest of Harwood has developed and the population trebled during the latter half of the 20th Century, the Hardy Mill community has survived with only the loss of the old mill and farm across the way and its name lives on into the Third Millennium AD with Hardy Mill Road. Here's hoping it remains that way for many years to come.

APPENDICES

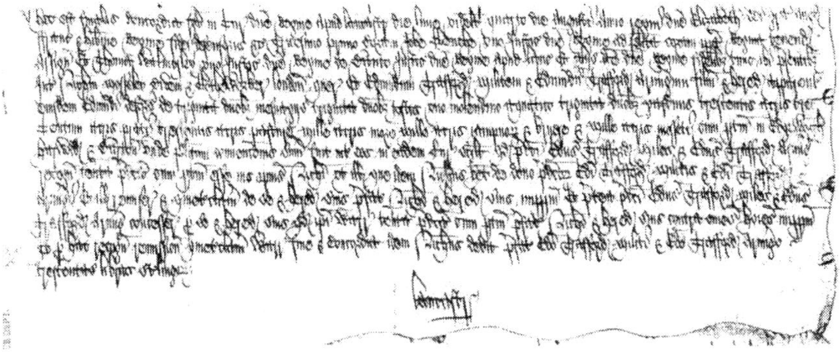

Manchester Local Studies M31/1/2/3 1589. Wilton Papers DDE 6/10

A1 FINAL CONCORD 4th August 1589

This is the final concord made in the Court of the lady the Queen at Lancaster on Monday, namely the fourth day of August in the thirty first year of the reign of the lady Elizabeth by the Grace of God Queen of England, France and Ireland, Defender of the Faith, etc. Before John Clenche, a Justice appointed to hold Pleas before the said Queen and Thomas Walmysley, a Justice of the Bench of the lady the Queen Justices of the lady the Queen at Lancaster and others faithful to the said lady the Queen then and there present Between Nicholas Mosslely citizen and clothmaker of London, plaintiff and Edmund Trafford, Knight and Edmund Trafford, Esquire, son and heir apparent of the said Edmund, deforciants concerning thirty two messuages, thirty two tofts, one water mill, thirty two gardens, three hundred acres of land, one hundred acres of meadow, three hundred acres of pasture, one thousand acres of moor, one thousand acres of heath and heather, and one thousand acres of moss land with appurtenances in Edgworth, Harwood and Barton whereupon a plea of covenant was summoned between them in the same court that is to say that the said Edmund Trafford, Knight and the said Edmund Trafford, Esquire, have acknowledged the said tenements with appurtenances to be the right of the said Nicholas as those which the said Nicholas had of the gift of the said Edmund Trafford, Knight and the said Edmund Trafford, Esquire and those they have remised and quitclaimed from them and their heirs to the said Nicholas and his heirs forever and moreover the said Edmund Trafford, Knight and the said Edmund Trafford, Esquire, have granted for themselves and their heirs that they will warrant the tenements and appurtenances to the said Nicholas and his heirs against all men forever and for this acknowledgement, quitclaim, warranty, fine and agreement the said Nicholas has given to the said Edmund Trafford, Knight and Edmund Trafford, Esquire, three hundred pounds sterling . Lancaster

A2 BOLTON JOURNAL October 30th, 1908

WINNOWING MACHINE AND FLAIL by J T Hargreaves

When the Hopwood family resided at Hardy Mill (cl840-1880) we (the villagers) had our own cabbage and turnip crops with carrots, beans, wheat and oats on many acres, and it used to be a pleasure to pass through the village in the harvest season, to see the harvesters at work among the corn, making the sheaves and piling them up into stooks to ripen and dry in the sun. Then came the carting away ready for the threshing machine which used to visit us once a year.

Grain growing in our village has an interesting history as is denoted by our having a cornmill driven by water power.

There were also interesting devices in those days. One was the winnowing machine and the other the threshing flail. The former used to separate the chaff from the grain after threshing, while the latter was used to separate the grain from the straw. I remember once going into a barn in Harwood when quite a lad and seeing a threshing flail at work. It consisted of a long stile about 4½ft long coupled by means of leather fastenings to another piece of wood 2½ft long, the shorter length being much thicker and heavier than the other. The heavier part was brought down on the sheaves of corn in the same manner that a blacksmith's striker brings down his sledgehammer on the heated iron, but care and practice were required to enable the man using the flail not to break the grains as they fell from the ears of corn.

A3 EXTRACT FROM THE WILL OF MEADOWCROFT HEATON 11th June, 1760

I Meadowcroft Heton of Harwood ... give and bequeath the profits arising out of all my lands for the space of ten Years from Mayday last past to bring up my two sons Charles and Thomas: after the end of the said term I also do give and bequeath my estate now lying at Nabfold in the said County together with my estate Isherwoods in Harwood and Harwood Meadows in Harwood in the said County unto my three sons John Heaton, Charles and Thomas share and share alike during John Heatons natural life: after his decease I do give and bequeath all the lands above mentioned to my two sons Charles and Thomas share and share alike ... I also do give and bequeath unto my daughter Margaret Burton my estate called the old Pit in Harwood in the said County during her natural Life: after her decease I do give and bequeath the said old Pit unto my grandsons Richard and Thomas Burton share and share alike ... I also do give and bequeath to my granddaughter Rachel Heton my three Houses in Bolton.

A4 BOLTON JOURNAL August 27th, 1909

CO-PARTNERY, TEA COMPANY ROW, HARWOOD by J T Hargreaves

The first co-operative store was opened in Toad Lane, Rochdale about the year 1844 by the Rochdale Pioneers. They were about 30 poor weavers most of whom were socialists of the Owen's School. Owen's ideas at that time were gaining considerable favour. The store seems to have been only a distributive one, buying and selling flour, butter, oatmeal and sugar. The ideas of Owen seem to have permeated into our own locality a few years after the system was made known and was taken up in a similar way by a group of industrious poor men who placed their small capital together with a view to developing some form of co-partnery.

What remains of it may be seen today in the name of Tea Company Row in Longsight, Harwood. It consists of a row of about 8 cottages with a shop at one end, and the inner portion of the house at the other end was specially built for one of the group for tailoring purposes. The ideas of this band of men were no doubt of the very highest order but their efforts do not seem to have met with the same success as those of Rochdale. The Harwood co-partnery would no doubt have been a production one as well as distributive.

A5 EXTRACT FROM THE WILL OF JOHN WALCH 24th November, 1819

I John Walch of Harwood ... give devise and bequeath unto my son David Walch All that messuage or dwelling house adjoining up to my Corn Mill situate at Hardy Mill in Harwood ... in the occupation of John Warburton as tenant thereof subject to the payment of a yearly ground rent of one pound to Alice Ormrod ... And also all those two other messuages or dwelling houses and plot of land thereto belonging and occupied therewith heretofore part of the Common Land in Harwood and now in the possession of James Scowcroft and John Scholes as tenants ... To hold the three messuages or dwelling houses, land and premises unto my son David Walch for and during all my estate term or interest therein and thereto upon the following Trusts that is to say Intrust that he .... shall receive and take the yearly rents, issues and profits from the three messuages and pay and apply the same into the proper hands of my daughter Margaret the wife of William Thweat during her natural life ... with the payment of the sum of Fifty Pounds to my son David Walch out of the first rents and profits ... I do also give and bequeath to my son David Walch all that corn mill, drying kiln, dam with the watercourses in Harwood ... And also all that messuage or dwelling house, shippon, outbuildings and premises with the appurtenancies thereto belonging situate in front of the said mill. And also an allotment or close of land lying on the south side of the road below Hardy Mill with the watercourses running through same.

A6 EXTRACT FROM THE WILL OF MARGARET THWEAT 13th March, 1830

Now I Margaret Thweat do hereby give devise and bequeath unto my brother David Walch ... All those three messuages or dwelling houses lands and premises so devised and bequeathed to him in trust for me by the Will of my father ... Subject to the payment of the yearly chief rent payable in respect of the messuage or dwelling house situate near Hardy Mill to Alice Ormrod her heirs and assigns and as to the remainder of the yearly rents and profits arising from the premises after payment of the yearly chief rent. It is my Will and mind that the same shall be paid yearly and every year to my husband William Thweat during his natural life.

A7 BOLTON JOURNAL OCTOBER 11th, 1907

OUD SACKS (SACHS) FACTORY IN HARWOOD by J T Hargreaves

There are people living today at four score years who, providing their memory served them right, could tell something about the history of the above, but whether the subject concerns their early days, or their parents, I am not at present able to say. However, not much appears to have been known about the man: he came into Harwood practically a stranger and seems to have disappeared quite as suddenly. After his little weaving shed had been doomed to failure (this was supposed to be due to domestic trouble) he left the district. The little shed was made of timber and contained about a dozen looms. It was situated in the field on the left hand side of the Well Studs entering from the Ruins end, now owned by the Trustees of David Walsh's Charity and then owned by David Walch, the corn miller, whose little corn mill was at work higher up the brook driven by a little wheel supplied by water from the old mill dam.

Passing over the ground, I find there is not much to be seen today of the arrangement that the old man made to carry on the work, except the little water fence which was formed by pitching stones in the bed of the brook to cause it to back up. From here the water was carried to the waterwheel by means of wooden troughs. There is also the old tunnel through which the overflow water passed after it left the by-wash in heavy and stormy weather into the original course of the stream. The by-wash itself - which was formed of a narrow neck of greensward backed up by a little stone wall, over which the water flowed - remained intact up to a few years ago, as also did the hole into which the water-wheel was fixed

A great many years ago, I used to hear the story told by the person who made the wheel, about an altercation between himself and the old gentleman as to how it should be constructed to make sure it would run satisfactorily: but Sachs had it his way, with the result that the wheel became loose on the shaft upon which it was mounted, so that when the water came down into the buckets it ceased to drive the machinery, and simply ran round the bar of iron upon which it ought to have been firmly fixed.

A8 BOLTON JOURNAL August 23rd, 1907

BRADSHAW, HARDY MILL AND AFFETSIDE By J T Hargreaves

...passing the Wesleyan Church and Walsh's Institute on Hardy Mill Road, at the footing of the hill to Nab Gate - which I am informed never had a gate, but is a corruption of Nab Gait on the way to Nab Fold - stands Hardy Mill through which still flows the little stream which once turned the millstones. The mounting block formed of disused millstones is still standing by the wayside. Lining the curve of the road here are the only tall poplars I know about in the district.

Opposite Hardy Mill is the one time residence of Charles Hopwood, who was for 20 years Chairman of the Board of Guardians. He worked the quarry at Brookfold Lane, a big bluff, heavily built figure of a man who could stand on the mounting block and by using his hands as a megaphone *'get a hustle'* on his men working a quarter of a mile away. In those days the huge stone slabs for cistern bottoms for which this quarry was noted had to be lifted by the laborious winding of a hand crane, and brawn and muscle held the places now occupied by steam and electricity. Hopwood must have been a man of some originality, for even at that time, when quiet colour and whitewash was almost universal he startled the community by having his house painted with scarlet vermillion at *'six bob a pound'*, as the local decorator informed me. Behind the house in a garden thick with flowering shrubs and fruit trees, runs an ever flowing well of iron impregnated water. Seen through an arbour of virginia creeper, it forms a lovely natural background for the photographer. It is a pleasant spot to while away the hours of a warm afternoon and as in addition, good and inexpensive teas are provided, there is no wonder that this has become a popular calling place.

A9 BOLTON JOURNAL November 27th, 1908

THE LAST LOCAL MAN-TRAP by 'Observer'

It is noteworthy that the poplar trees at Hardy Mill planted by the late Daniel Hopwood about 1880 are a feature of the locality, standing sentinel like in their regular line along the highroad. Where they are planted was originally the vegetable garden of the late Mr Hopwood. He also planted two or three in his kitchen garden at Hardy Mill House and a fine yew tree, together with a sycamore or two. It may not be out of place to record here that probably the Harwood district was the last place locally in which a man-trap was used. Mr Hopwood had one made by his smith at the stone quarry and set it in his garden near the poplar trees because he kept missing his cabbages. The story runs that it caught a man - the policeman - and ever afterwards its fame was so noised abroad right through the district that the necessity for its use passed away. This trap, which is still in existence was discovered by the writer when he resided in the district.

REFERENCES

R1 *'1257 Avina de Samlesbury acknowledged the right of Robert de Hampson and Margery his wife to a mill and eight oxgangs of land in Breightmet'.* Victoria County History of Lancashire Breightmet.

R2 The Great Inquest of King John in 1212 details land-holdings and knights' service liabilities of the tenants-in-chief. The Book of Fees PRO Kew.

R3 Subinfeudation into smaller estates created fractions of knights' service, which meant that several tenants became responsible for the service of one knight. This could be achieved by providing service in rotation, but the services were later commuted to monetary values which developed into fiscal units.

R4 Final Concords were conveyances of land or property by means of a legal action with the final agreement being recorded in the King's Court. The actions were often brought to break an entail, which was a restriction on the line of descent. After 1300 the conveyances were normally fictitious with approximate acreages and meaningless values, and often no money changed hands.

R5 Indenture Knotts Estate Papers, Mr John Calderbank, Hoyles Fold. An Indenture is a deed with two or more parties and was originally written twice (or more) on a single piece of parchment. The document was then cut through with an indented (or wavy) line (or lines) for identification purposes and each party kept one section.

R6 Matthew Harrison listed in Subsidy Roll 1622, died 1633: Henry Haworth married Elizabeth Haslam and died 1623: Raufe Higson married Margaret Sannderson 1597: Lawrence Horrocks died 1652: Edward Greenhalgh married Issabel Fogge 1587 and died 1624: Raufe Higson and John Brooke, gentlemen of Harwood, were jurors at the Inquisition post mortem of Rowland Mosley, Lord of the Manor of Manchester in 1617.

R7 Several selective lists of Harwood inhabitants in the 1600s are available; PROTESTATION RETURNS 1641. A census of all male inhabitants of eighteen and over who were required to pledge their allegiance to the Protestant Religion, King Charles I and Parliament. HEARTH TAX 1662-74, Occupiers of houses worth more than twenty shillings a year paid two shillings per hearth. Others were not liable. POLL TAX 1678. Levied to finance the war with France. One shilling per person over sixteen; two shillings per servant. People considered too poor were exempt from payment.

R8 Knotts: Knotts Estate Papers. Mr John Calderbank.
Heights: Lancashire Record Office. Ref QDD 21/20.
Greenhalgh Fold: Bolton Libraries. Archives Ref ZZ/52/1.
Brookfold: Hulme Deeds No 108 & 109 Chetham's Library.

R9 In 1630, Adam Mort of Astley held a messuage and fulling mill of Edward Mosley, Lord of Manchester. VCH Harwood 12.

R10 Most of the Ainsworth family estate seems to have been acquired by Giles Aynesworth by about 1600 including Oakenbottom Cornmill (held of the Earl of Derby) and fourteen messuages etc in Breightmet and Harwood (VCH). In 1615 he purchased Brookfold, Harwood for £38 from the five yeomen trustees of Harwood. (Hulme Deed 108, Chetham's Library). His daughter Katherine married Richard Banastre of Bolton and they lived at Oakenbottom in Breightmet township. The grand-daughter of Giles Ainsworth from this union, Christine, married William Hulme from Reddish and in 1631 they produced great-grandson, William Hulme Jnr. During the mid-1600s, William Hulme Jnr acquired extensive estates mainly in Lancashire and Cheshire and in 1655 purchased the whole of the Ainsworth estate. He leased Brookfold to the occupant, William Brooke in 1664 (Hulme Deed No 112). When he died in 1691 he left an endowment to Brazenose College, Oxford of £64 a year which had escalated by the mid 1800s to £5000.

R 11 Edgworth and District Agricultural Society 1908.

R12 The Heatons of Deane. Edmund R Heaton 2000.

R13 The Heatons of Heaton-under-Forest. John Heaton Partington 1903 Bolton Library Archives B920 Hea.

R14 Bolton Library Archives ZAL 20. On the Enclosure of Bolton Moor in 1792, John Albinson (1775-1854) was appointed Surveyor and Clerk to the Trustees at the age of 18. He remained in the position for 50 years and over 1300 of his plans and documents are retained in Bolton Archives. He was an avid collector of books and paintings.

R15 The acre measures 40 rods (furlong) x 4 rods (chain) = 160 square rods. Edward I ruled the standard rod (perch or pole) to be 5½yds but local variations persisted into the 1800s. The Cheshire acre was mainly used south of the Ribble and the Lancashire acre to the north.
Statute Acre - rod 5½yds - acre (160 x $5½^2$) = 4840 yds^2.
Cheshire Acre - rod 8 yds - acre (160 x 8^2) = 10,240 yds^2
Lancashire Acre - rod 7 yds - acre (160 x 7^2) = 7840 yds^2

R16 The Enclosure of Harwood Commons. J J Francis 1990 TLHS

RI7 Field names: Carr - marshy land; Hey - enclosed field; Croft - enclosed meadow adjacent to a building; Close - field enclosed from the open fields or commons; Shut - field that could be closed off: Roy - probably from rye.

R 18 Bowkhouse: Farmers were encouraged to bleach their own cloth before chemical bleaching was developed in the late 1700s. Bowking was the initial process of removing fats and starches by boiling the cloth in a solution of the ash of burnt beech, oak, ash, nettles, thorns, thistles or hemlock. The cloth was then washed, neutralized by soaking in buttermilk, washed again, and then spread out in the sunlight to *'whiten'*. Both buttermilk and *'white ash'* were rural products.

R19 Bradshaw Chapel II. J J Francis 1998 TLHS

R20 The Sayings & Doings of Rev James Folds 1879. Joseph Dodson Greenhalgh

R21 The Scowcroft Diaries - Scowcroft Family. Samuel Scowcroft (1839-1914), a shopkeeper from Bradshaw, kept a diary from 1861 to 1910 and later added items (with comments) from 1791 to 1880 from a diary of Jim o' Charles (James Lee 1780-1860) and Tim o' Charles (Thomas Lee 1807-1880), both of Brookfold Lane, Harwood.

R22 The Scowcroft Family Tree and History. Arthur W Critchley, Ontario, Canada via Mrs Lillian Tinsley, Hawkshaw.

Acknowledgments

Special thanks to Mrs Jean Vickers for providing invaluable information from her previous researches: Mr James J Francis for his informative help throughout the study: Mr Edward Hardy for contriving the *'artists'* impression of the cornmill: Mr Kevin Campbell, Bolton Libraries Archivist for translation of the 1589 Final Concord.

Also thanks to Mr John Calderbank, Hoyles Fold Farm, Harwood, Mr Leonard Young, Harwood and Mr Alfred & Mrs Barbara Partington, Hardy Mill for making available early deeds: to the Partingtons for providing access and constructive information: the Trustees of David Walsh's Charity for access to papers of Hardy Mill and Chairman John Blackburn for help in searching records: the staffs of Chetham's Library, Bolton Library Archives, Lancashire Record Office, GM County Record Office, Hertfordshire County Archives, the Public Record Office, Kew and the British Library, London.

In addition, thanks to all those other people too numerous to name, who have offered information and advice during the study. JFH

Made in the USA
Las Vegas, NV
11 April 2026

45201017R00042